MIMESIS
INTERNATIONAL

SOCIOLOGY
n. 7

FIAMMETTA FANIZZA
MARCO OMIZZOLO

CAPORALATO
An Authentic Agromafia

MIMESIS
INTERNATIONAL

This book has been published with the contribution of 'Bando pubblicazioni scientifiche 2018' Università di Foggia -Dipartimento di Studi Umanistici.

© 2018 – Mimesis International
www.mimesisinternational.com
e-mail: info@mimesisinternational.com

Book series: *Sociology*, n. 7

Isbn: 9788869772191

© MIM Edizioni Srl
P.I. C.F. 0241937030

Cover image: Tomatoes greenhouse in Ragusa, Sicily, one of the center of caporalato phenomenon.

TABLE OF CONTENTS

INTRODUCTION

The goal of this essay is to analyze the phenomenon of agromafias. Focusing in particular on *caporalato*, the idea is to define the dynamics and effects produced by criminal networks that in Italy adopt approaches and methods to exploit immigrants in the production and harvest of agricultural products.

Examining the logic and processes behind the globalization of the farmlands and the internationalization of business relationships between Italian mafias and foreigners, this text deals with the topic of the agromafias' role and analyzes some matters related to the deregulation of the agricultural market as well as the general crisis of the agroindustries.

As regards *caporalato* practices, the data concerning the transformation undergone by the territories most exposed to this agromafia phenomenon opens up the discussion on the enslavement of immigrant agricultural labourers and territorial segregation practices. Based on the data collected and elaborated by the authors during the course of studies and research conducted over the last ten years, *caporalato* has become a methodological instrument for evaluating the complex relationship between the agromafias' power and the operational conditions of Italy's local economies. Furthermore, given the number of available resources regarding related events and investigations of a penal nature, the examination of the circumstances that lead Europol to classify certain Italian regions as criminal hubs represents an opportunity to realize a comparative evaluation of the lack of investments, poor use of public resources, and delayed local and national development in Italy.

Regarding the topic of weak or delayed local development, the thesis proposed by the authors begins by studying the logic behind the installation, organization, and expansion of agricultural organizations. By focusing on precarious housing, a condition that keeps the cost of manual day labourers very low, this essay critically considers how the ghettos dispersed throughout the Italian countryside (particularly in the South) allow the criminal apparatus of the agromafias to expand. The ghettos are logistical bases used to subjugate the immigrants and thus compromise agriculture and inhibit the growth of local economies by limiting their potential within the agricultural sector both in Italy and the European Union.

Through an examination of the logic behind the installation, organization, and expansion of agricultural organizations, the authors explore elements of the extremely pervasive criminal network that determines productive trends of entire agricultural departments and as a result is capable of conditioning the growth and development of communities and entire social systems. Thus the study of the logic behind the installation, organization, and expansion of agricultural organizations is the lens that shows how violence and illegality undermine the rules imposed by society's cultural code, which should theoretically prevent the accumulation of illicit capital and prevent the agromafia from normalizing its effects on "social capital" and "social forms". On the contrary, given that the cultural code has been undermined, violence and illegality allow for the emergence of a structural criminal model that is able to organize social, economic, political, and cultural aspects. Therefore the goal of this essay is to provoke critical thought on the matter in order to identify the epistemological context suitable to understanding the complexity of the issue. Indeed, since these themes have an impact even on an international level, the identification of a criminal agromafia model is an opportunity to study the relationship between this model and the methods with which political, economic, and social contexts choose meaningful objectives. This model is in continuous evolution, and its ramifications are ascribable to its mafia-like ability to install in a territory and are thus attributable to the inability and/ or unpreparedness of the managing political classes to manage public affairs and exercise their public office. Therefore the goal of this book is to highlight the risks to the "social sector". In addition to the topics addressed, the authors intend to denounce the dangerous socio-cultural drifting that mafia-like criminal organizations are creating on an Italian and international level. This dangerous drifting has the power to contaminate the role of political and economic institutions and set up a scenario in which commercial and economic aspects are dominated by a culture of illegality that realizes the paradox of the social and political consecration of impunity. In a cultural climate so conditioned by the criminal mindset that exploitation and violence are legitimized, legal practices put in place to manage economic affairs are called into question, especially when public resources are involved. Impunity can even obtain some social validation, especially when it manages to present itself in juxtaposition with the static nature of institutions and the dynamic nature of criminal organizations.

From a political and social perspective, this juxtaposition leads to the temptation to realize a cultural metamorphosis whose speculative goals allow new partnerships to adopt unprecedented forms of support and reciprocal exchange. The authors consider these new partnerships with the auspice that a different network of relationships interwoven with different "pieces" of society can cause illegality to be stigmatized as a dysfunctional resource and allow "social capital" to re-establish its characteristic traits and distinctive roles.

1.
WHEN WE TALK ABOUT *CAPORALATO*, WE ARE TALKING ABOUT AN AGROMAFIA

FIAMMETTA FANIZZA

I In Italy, particularly in the country's southern regions (Sicily, Calabria, Apulia, and Lazio), the entire process of growing, harvesting, and producing agricultural products is founded upon the exploitation of manual labour. Over the course of the years, this practice has consolidated its power and become a bona fide system. This system of exploitation, called *caporalato* in Italian, consists of illegally controlling and managing all phases of growing, harvesting, and producing agricultural products. The gangmasters, called *caporali*, are part of fully-functioning criminal organizations that use mafia-like methods to impose rules and consequently condition the trends of the agricultural seasons as well as the fruit and vegetable markets.

Although these statements may seem excessive and perhaps alarming, they are the result of numerous investigations[1] that have confirmed these facts year after year, sketching a worrisome picture that involves many Italian regions. In addition to attesting to crimes, these investigations have

---

1 Among others, we refer to those conducted by the Italian *Carabinieri* police force in "Operation Salib" in 2005 when, through broad-spectrum investigations, law enforcement was able to defeat a gang led by Albanians that branched out through Calabria, Sicily, Apulia, Lombardy, Piedmont, Tuscany, and Emilia-Romagna. The group's activity was primarily dedicated to international drug and weapons smuggling but also included enslavement, facilitating illegal immigration, and exploiting prostitutes. Operating through still unknown connections and collaboration with the Sibari clans within 'Ndrangheta, the group used some commercial farms in Apulia as their logistic bases.
These activities periodically occupy law enforcement as seen in a February 2018 operation that engaged the G.I.C.O. (Organized Crime Investigation Group) in Trento (in the northwest) and the police headquarters in Foggia (in southwestern Italy). The operation led to the seizure of 1,000 kilograms of drugs from Morocco that was to be sold in Italy and Spain after being rehydrated in a large farmhouse in the Melfi area of Basilicata (a region in southern Italy that borders with Apulia). Based on what is known at this point, the drugs found in northern Italy were intended to be sold in Trento and Turin (in the north). Therefore, contrary to popular belief, it is a problem that permeates the entire country and is not limited to the southern regions.

above all revealed just how extensive and incisive the *caporali*'s power is. Their power is absolute and explained in their ability to determine harvest trends, the labourers' employment conditions, and not least, the retail price of products. It is thanks to the results of these investigations that we can affirm the following:

- The *caporali* select and hire agricultural labourers;
- The *caporali* establish the number of hours in a work day and the corresponding wages for a day labourer;
- The *caporali* negotiate production rules with agriculturists and consequently take control of commercial farms;
- The *caporali* decide how much to produce and how to distribute the products in wholesale markets;
- The *caporali* not only stipulate agreements with Italy's MMR (Mass Market Retailers), but they also dictate the conditions of the market provisions both in Italy and abroad.

In light of the fact that *caporalato* is capable of controlling production processes in the vast majority of agricultural sectors, it is possible to affirm that it is truly a regime. In fact, since the *caporali*'s power is by now so consolidated and engrained that the alimentary industries are subjected to their decisions, it is now more than ever advantageous to be aware of this phenomenon and understand it in light of the commercial processes caused by the so-called *globalization of the farmlands*.

The ability to influence the agriculturists' decisions and penetrate the dynamics that govern many areas of the sector represents an evolution due to the effect of organized criminality in agriculture. Whereas in the past the illegal activity of the *caporali* primarily consisted of organizing the transportation of the labourers from the camps where they live to the fields, today their contribution is much more vast, involving more subjects and "skills". The fact that every phase, action, and intervention in production, elaboration, distribution, and sale is controlled by the *caporali* means that they control not only the labourers but, in many Italian businesses, also the agriculturists. Therefore, in the past *caporalato* almost exclusively limited the workers' freedom but did not condition market trends, whereas today it conditions the cycles of the numerous phases of agricultural manufacturing and restricts the producers and industries, who are more or less aware of the situation and accept the *caporali*'s power, or at least tolerate being part of a production mechanism hinged on mafia-like practices and methods. Hence, while thirty years ago the *caporale* was a figure that "collaborated" with agriculturists, today he is a figure that limits their actions, influencing the situations in which they operate their businesses. Thus, the *caporale* is no longer an individual who assists the owner and helps him manage his agro-industry by maintaining the manual labourers, who are recruited daily, in extreme subordination all from within a culture saturated by legacies linked to the latifundium tradition. Today the *caporale* has taken upon himself many of the pertinent functions of the businessman's role and thus intimidates, albeit with many different methods and effects, both the labourers and the commercial farm owners.

Before going into the relevant characteristics and dynamics, it is of the utmost importance to define the *caporalato* system as an agromafia, or in other words a criminal regime that utilizes an organized hierarchical network that operates throughout the national territory. Since, as is easily deduced from these brief arguments, this definition is a necessity and not merely a lexical choice, the principle objective of this volume is to demonstrate the serious consequences brought about by *caporalato* as a regime that exploits labourers, illegally accumulates wealth, and compromises economic growth and territorial development on a local, national, and at times international level.

II   The need to define *caporalato* as an agromafia is linked first of all to the gravity of this phenomenon and the urgent need to stop considering the exploitive practices upon which it is founded as territorially sporadic and delimited. Furthermore, this urgent need can be seen as an opportunity to relaunch the agro-industry economy and promote meaningful, local development concerning both commodities and social growth. Thus, before going into the explanation of how *caporalato* is organized, developed, and expanded, we must concentrate our attention on the link between the exploitation of manual labour and economic and social impoverishment. Referring specifically to the practices of segregation and enslavement that are regularly utilized by the *caporali* and which are by now, I would say, implicit from an etymological point of view, the connection assumes a functional nature. Revealing the correlation between the cruelty with which the labourers are treated and the progressive economic marginalization that afflicts the geographic contexts in which the *caporali* act allows us to establish the correspondence between *caporalato* and an entire group of crimes that for simplicity's sake will be referred to in this text under the category of "fraud and evasion". The pressing need is that the phenomenon of *caporalato* be dealt with systematically and with tools whose approach and methods foresee adequate action regardless of the working and living conditions of the labourers. Although these are greatly and dramatically evident, to eradicate *caporalato* it is preliminarily indispensable to study the economic and social weight that economic marginalization produces on the different (local, national, and international) contexts. Along with identifying and explaining the (historical, cultural, etc.) causes, it is therefore just as important to demonstrate that *caporalato* prospers in conditions of economic marginalization.

Even though almost all the studies carried out in the last ten years have highlighted the nexus between the presence of agromafias and stunted development, they have overwhelmingly focused on the cruelties suffered by human beings – above all immigrants – and have failed to carefully, quantitatively examine the social damage that *caporalato* generates. Nonetheless, in an absolutely involuntary way, these studies have allowed the debate on human rights to obscure the debate on economic underdevelopment and lack of productive growth. In other words, they have allowed a certain "cultural tolerance" to delay – and sometimes even prevent, as is the case in many areas of northern Italy – the spreading of awareness. This awareness is important in light of the outcomes of the operations carried out by law enforcement and as a result of the increase in police reports filed for:

- Tax evasion;
- Income tax evasion;
- Fraud.

These are particular cases of fraud committed by agriculturists that harm the Italian government and the European Union, which annually distributes grants that are legally collected by those in the agricultural business in many areas in Italy. These fiscal crimes, so to speak, allow *caporalato* to misappropriate financial resources and further profit from putting people's lives at risk. Consequently, they amplify the economic advantage derived from illegalities. Indeed *caporalato* prospers thanks to the absence of a "culture of legality". The latter results in a conditioned and resigned society in which any kind of reaction against *caporalato* is very difficult to put into practice. For this reason, entire geographical territories are subjected to the prejudice which derives from being assigned the stigma of criminality, proving a competitive advantage for the *caporali* who reign and exercise almost a monopoly on agricultural management and most of the agroindustries. In summary, cultural weakness sets the stage for an environment where the mafia is allowed to determine the situations and destinies of people and countries.

Unpaid tributes and taxes as well as the illegal or fraudulent collection of grants are situations that occur because of the absence of an adequate business culture. Like the causes, the elements are difficult to trace and decipher. Contributing to the progressive repudiation of business culture are multiple factors that are nevertheless indicative, on the one hand, of the objective difficulty of doing business in a context where criminality is present and, on the other hand, of a resistance to promote innovations in the methods of doing business.

In general, the situation of Italian commercial farms is as varied as it is difficult to codify the productive practices. In view of the complex agricultural traditions, cultivation methods, and productive procedures, the common denominator is an increasing need for intensive practices, at times so invasive as to be introduced without taking into account climatic and seasonal variables. Even though their unconditional adoption is often paradoxical, these practices are dictated by market demands, which overlook changing environmental conditions and requires methods that supplant cultural uncertainty with economic flexibility in an effort to guarantee paradoxically the predictableness of the yield. Confusing the parameters of agricultural productivity with those of mass industrial productivity obviously requires mechanized processes. Since the greatest drawback is precisely that it is impossible to control unforeseen factors and maintain control over climatic and seasonal variables, this mechanization focuses on the exploitation of manual labour as the only truly flexible resource that is available regardless of possible environmental glitches.

Unlike popular belief that is content to describe the Italian agricultural situation using unchanged images from the past, the Italian farmlands in both northern and southern Italy have for years been implementing radical changes that link the agroindustries with the globalized system of capitalistic accumulation. Essentially these changes involve the following:

- Large infrastructural endowments;
- The development of services for the organization of local rural systems;
- Demographic movements.

Economically speaking and from a socio-territorial perspective, the phenomenon of the globalization of the farmlands identifies a process of morphological restructuring of rural and productive areas dictated by the expansion of the chains belonging to the Italian MMR (Mass Market Retailers). With ultra-territorial preconditions and rules that at times are absolutely disrespectful of environmental, landscape, cultural, and even economic resources, the main goal of the globalization of the farmlands is to connect production centres with those of consumption. To this end, they support the globally organized project for economic growth, and the connection between production centres and consumption centres subjugates every other management philosophy, becoming the exclusive and, so to speak ontological, goal. This paradigm imposes a new course on agricultural production; the connection between production and consumption becomes a measure to appraise the market, or rather to assign value to goods, capital, investments, know-how, and last but not least human capital. As a parameter to put into practice the idea of economic growth, the connection between production centres and consumption centres ends up penalizing the agricultural sector, subjecting it to a process of capitalistic acceleration founded on the imposition of a monopoly regulated by the economic doctrine derived from the most intransigent and unrestrained free-trade and laissez-faire principles. In agriculture, this doctrine remains linked to the dogma of the greatest profit obtainable at the lowest possible cost. Therefore, in the plains and near the coasts first and foremost and also in hilly and alpine areas, the principle of the greatest profit becomes an authentic archetype.

Against this backdrop, the goal of maximizing profits and reducing costs depends on the availability of flexible manual labour that is "on-call" so to speak. With the rise of indispensable regulatory criteria for the market, easily obtained and readily available manual labour is guaranteed by the contingents of immigrants that arrive by sea from Africa and Asia. As we will see shortly, migratory fluxes assume a crucial role for entire agricultural production chains. Distinguished and subdivided by ethnicity, the immigrants become the load-bearing axis of the new model of agricultural business. Their presence allows production costs to be contained and businesses to maintain and reintroduce proprietorial management models. Even more than a preliminary condition dictated by the competition, the exploitation of manual labour has thus become an implied presupposition that is at the same time a structural prerequisite for rural economy in the 21st century.

Above all as an indirect consequence of the EU's economic and financial support, over approximately the last twenty years the new course of business has reintroduced atmospheres and conditions of the latifundium tradition. In addition to these, a class of small and medium business owners has developed, many of whom have reconverted after failing in the tertiary sector or as a consequence of the decline of industrialized processes both in the southern regions and in the fragile, central areas of Italy. The presence of a "new agriculturist" is determined by the increase in demand for manual labour, especially foreign labourers, who are willing to work in any conditions. In a context where adherence to the rules of the market and the protection of the labourers is systematically waived or even disregarded, the demand for day labourers has become the thermometer for measuring the competition. The focus on personal economic gain, at the expense of immigrant agricultural labourers, and the exploitation of all available resources prevents economic growth and employment goals. Since the way of doing business has become purely a method for capitalistic gain, wellbeing is evaluated in terms of personal profit. When business does not take into consideration social aspects, human capital becomes merely a cost to cut as much as possible, and consequently the labourers are paid less and less. Instead of having societal value, business consists of individual goals, which sustain and are sustained by a culture of individualism. Individual profit and undue enrichment become a sort managing philosophy.

Paradoxical and in violation of the most elementary and fundamental principles of the free market, the situation has become one in which personal enrichment at all costs has become the end goal. The pervading individualistic mentality sacrifices the collective wellbeing, and the deregulation of the market compromises business and produces impoverishment. Consequently, in addition to environmental impoverishment and diversified forms of productive dispersion, they have become the style of a way of doing business that produces no positive effect with regard to social wellbeing or in terms of expansion and development. Therefore, it is probably thanks to excessive individualism that criminal organizations prosper and economic progress involves the exploitation of all types of resources (natural, human, and environmental).

III   The backdrop that emerges as a result of the globalization of the farmlands shows the following:
- Masses of poor oppressed immigrants subjected to exploitation and violence;
- The development of a new form of "farmers without land", as the protagonist of transnational migrations.

At the heart of both of these are issues of poverty and human rights, calling into question the direct, indirect, and widespread outcomes of globalization.

To adequately develop this complex topic we must address two problems that are just as intricate: the exploitation of manual labour and what is essentially the enslavement of immigrant agricultural labourers.

Since *caporalato* is a regime financed in part by unpaid contributions to social security and taxes as well as the illegal or fraudulent collection of grants distributed primarily by the EU, the living conditions of these new "farmers without land" are a decisive variable with regard to the prosperity of *caporalato*. Therefore, after having demonstrated the nexus between the misappropriation of public resources, *caporalato*, and the globalization of the farmlands, it is inevitable that we should focus on the topic of the segregation of the labourers into rural ghettos and makeshift camps. This entails violations of human and social rights as well as the economic exploitation of entire territories. What essentially allows the *caporalato* regime to thrive and prosper is the fact that the immigrant labourers are completely deprived of personal freedom in the Italian farmlands.

Particularly in southern Italy (specifically in Sicily, Calabria, Apulia, Campania, and Lazio), the possibility of exercising control over agricultural production depends on the unlimited availability of immigrant day labourers who, having reached Italy in search of a better future, are introduced into the productive mechanism with no possibility of professional growth[2]. The mechanism hinges on the fact that the labourers are forced to accept inhumane living conditions that basically correspond with their enslavement[3].

Caporalato is founded upon the deprivation of personal freedom through establishing work days rarely comprised of fewer than 12 hours and confining the labourers to ghettos or camps located a great distance from urban centres. Forced to live far away from the nearest town and divided up according to ethnicity and religious beliefs, the immigrants that arrive in Italy – the vast majority having landed on the coasts of Sicily – normally end up confined to dilapidated and often unstable rural buildings.

Their segregation and limited personal freedom is inescapable. Since the ghettos are isolated and illegal, the immigrants are not able to integrate or interact with local populations regardless of factors such as their nationality (African, Bulgarian, or Romanian) or the more or less favourable cultural environment. In other words, despite the conditions that characterize the area

---

2   Ambrosini M. (2005). *Sociologia delle migrazioni*. Bologna: il Mulino.
3   As early as 2008, a study carried out by Doctors Without Borders confronted the phenomenon and pointed out the gravity of the situation. Cfr., Medici Senza Frontiere, (2008) *Una stagione all'inferno*, http://archivio.medicisenzafrontiere. it/allegati/pubblicazioni/rapporti/una_stagione_all_inferno.pdf.

surrounding the ghettos, which are generally located in rural communities or on the outskirts of small or medium-size urban centres, integration has become an extremely remote possibility for the immigrants both for logistical reasons and because the *caporali* prohibit it. In order to avoid drawing attention to the illegal and inhumane working and living conditions, the *caporali* must hide their activities as well as the immigrant workers.

The working and living conditions of the immigrant day labourers call to mind some of the criticisms of the industrial era during the first social investigations of the 19th century by Friedrich Engels, Frédéric Le Play, and Charles Booth. It is alarming to see the similarities between the urban working class studied by Marx and Engels and this new rural working class. Like the awful working class neighbourhoods of the Industrial Revolution, the ghetto residents are hidden out of sight, almost as if "inexistent". Similar to the first English factory workers, foreign labourers have run-down accommodations and insufficient wages: recalling Engels's thoughts, they are the lowest paid workers whose wages decrease each day and who lose the strength to combat their conditions of misery, filth, and disease[4].

Required to pay between 25 and 100 euros a month for a place to sleep, the immigrants live with their compatriots without plumbing, running water, or electricity. Deprived of legal documents, they are in fact enslaved.

Just as they are "invisible" to their hosting communities, immigrant labourers who live in the ghettos are practically "invisible" even to their employers. Paradoxically, in fact, they are invisible to many of the agriculturists that accept, tolerate, or in some cases even benefit from the ghetto system.

Although it is possible to hypothesize that the *caporali* exercise a certain amount of control over the owners of commercial farms, probably forcing them to accept their involvement, it is plausible to imagine that, in the end, *caporalato* is seen as a way to simplify work relationships: the agriculturists pay the labourers' dues to the *caporali*, who hand them out after having subtracted their "commission". This way the *caporali* manage and organize the preparatory phases of agricultural work, relieving the agriculturist of a series of tasks and worries. Summarily the *caporali* provide protection and thus guarantee safety regarding the management of the labour and the farmer's revenue.

---

4   Engels F. (2011). *La situazione della classe operaia in Inghilterra: in base a osservazioni dirette e fonti autentiche* (Milano: Edizioni Lotta Comunista, pp. 88-90).

Moreover, as a result of the devastating *deregulation* of workers' rights, the absence of a solid business model leaves the commercial farmers in a position of weakness. As illustrated by numerous new reports, agricultural businesses are left in a state of anomie, which allows land owners to abdicate their business role, or rather to somehow transfer it to the *caporali*.

Evidently, entrusting the *caporali* with recruiting, hiring, and transporting the labourers relieves the agriculturist of responsibilities and managerial worries and definitively causes them to lose sight of their business's ultimate goal. Essentially since the *caporali*'s involvement reduces business risk, the business loses its specific mission and becomes identified with the individual agriculturist's profit. This erroneous way of causing individual and personal benefit to coincide with potential profits condemns the entire agricultural industry merely to survive and certainly not to grow economically or commercially.

Furthermore, given the vast and widespread nature of *caporalato* in the farmlands, there is no doubt as to whether or not the agriculturist is in fact ignorant of the *caporalato* regime. It seems rather unfathomable that the agriculturist does not gain anything from this regime. It is also rather difficult to believe that agriculturist is ignorant of the violence and oppression that the labourers who work on the farm are subjected to. In sum, the agriculturist ought to be considered in more or less indirect complicity with the *caporali*. Above all, the hypothesis that the agriculturist is unaware does not hold water when one considers the difference in treatment and payment that he adopts in violation of the terms of contract. For example, in the province of Foggia, an agricultural city in Apulia, world leader in the production of peeled tomatoes, daily wages are set at 48 euros per day, which is defined as 6.5 hours of work. However, it is the "custom" that the agriculturist pays a maximum of 36 euros[5] per 12-hour work day. Moreover, since the immigrant labourers receive piece rate pay and the *caporali* distribute their daily wages, the labourer only receives 25 of the 36 euros. That is not yet the net sum. In fact, from those 25 euros the *caporali* deduct the expenses of transportation to and from the fields in addition to other items including the following:

---

5   Labour unions have long declared that in the agricultural sector 60% of working hours are paid under the table. According to these organizations, the undeclared work involves more than 50% of manual labour and approximately 30% of the sector's GDP. It is a parallel universe in which immigrants represent 25% of the total number of undeclared workers. Cfr., Agenzia di Stampa DIRE, "Sicurezza, fra paura e bisogno di immigrazione", supplemento al numero 343 del 10 dicembre 2008, pag. 15.

- Living expenses (a sandwich and water at work; food and other essential supplies in the ghettos where the *caporali* manage the shops and eateries);
- Water for personal hygiene (in the ghettos individuals must pay even for the use of portable chemical toilets);
- Electricity (for example, to recharge cell phones, an indispensable item supplied by the *caporali* so that the labourers are available at any time);
- Sometimes drugs, which are "useful" in that they help the workers endure the physically exhausting work.

These expenses significantly reduce the wages so that at the end of the day each labourer has about 10-12 euros left.

Just as it is right to ask oneself if the agriculturist ought to be considered an accomplice to the *caporali* and perhaps even in some cases the instigator of these despicable methods of exploitation[6], one must also ask how the regime of ghetto systems manages to pass unobserved by law enforcement. In brutally evident contradiction to their institutional mission, local law enforcement appears to "tolerate" *caporalato* in that they seem "resigned" to this inevitable "reality" that it is a "local endemic tradition". Almost as if they belonged to another reality and social dimension, the ghettos are treated as if they were free-trade zones where any crime is a "matter between immigrants." These matters however involve even the natives since prostitution and the selling of drugs are thriving businesses, which significantly contribute to and increase the business volume of *caporalato*.

The diversifying of illegal business that occurs within the ghettos transforms the immigrant labourers into innocent protagonists in a universe of lawlessness. Rotating around agricultural work is this circuit of illegal business, which some time ago branched out to include extortion and racketeering, which seem to be the new methods of human exploitation. Sooner or later it will be necessary to study the phenomenon of the constant presence of immigrant mendicants outside of Italian supermarkets and shopping centres. In other words, the phenomenon and profitability of the exploitation of foreign mendicants is coming soon.

---

6   Leogrande A. (2008), *Uomini e caporali. Viaggio tra i nuovi schiavi nelle campagne del Sud,* Mondadori, Milano.

2.
THE ITALIAN AGROMAFIA CHAIN AND ITS TERRITORIAL ROOTING

Marco Omizzolo

I   The extension of the areas of influence and rooting of the mafias also to some parts of the national territory historically considered immune, with particular reference to the northern regions of the country, must induce in favour of analysis aimed at understanding the modalities that characterize the attitude beyond the traditional geographical boundaries, together with the criminal alliances that they can establish in association with subjects of the economic, political and administrative world of the country[1]. A thesis that is supported by an increasing number of experts, magistrates, researchers, who detect a growing awareness of the territorial expansion of the mafias (from Liguria to Piedmont, from Lombardy to Emilia Romagna, from Friuli Venezia Giulia to Valle d'Aosta). The so-called "mafias in motion" tend to determine, in the body governing even territorial, in front of the clear manifestation of the mafia clan, an "identity" or "simplistic" reaction such as the adoption of security laws containing manifestly repressive provisions, to be followed a "cultural" approach tending to exclude the occurrence of territorial settlements. It is a form of indirect denial that is very dangerous and that characterizes the territorial realities of the north of the country but also the international one. The process of expansion and rooting of the mafias in Italy sees in the Italian law of 1956, defined as the "coerced stays", its turning point. In fact, it established against a person,

---

1   The Aemilia process concerning the rooting of the 'ndrangheta in Emilia Romagna is emblematic. The convictions at first instance on October 31, 2018 come after more than two years of hearings have sanctioned the existence of a 'ndrangheta association that the District Anti-Mafia Directorate of Bologna considers operating since 2004. It is a partnership believed to be linked to the Grande Aracri clan of Cutro (Crotone), with its epicenter in Reggio Emilia. The trial aimed to hit the 'ndrangheta entrepreneur. According to the investigators, the group's objective has been acquired or indirectly the management and control of economic activities, also in the works for the earthquake of 2012, as well as obtaining public and private tenders for the elections from 2007 to 2012 in the provinces of Parma and Reggio Emilia.

often a member of the mafia, the obligation to reside in a different place than the one of origin and rooted in his criminal affairs, decided by the magistracy, for a certain period of time, as a preventive measure. The basic idea was to stem the social danger of criminals, frequently a member of the mafia, through their transfer to other areas or regions, imagining that this meant their isolation. Among those who could be subjected to this regime there were *"habitually committed to criminal trafficking"* or *"offending or endangering the physical or moral integrity of minors, health, safety or public tranquility"*.

In 1965, with the law n. 575, for the first time, the mafia and mobsters words are introduced into the Italian legal system and precise provisions are ordered against it. The suspects of belonging to the various mafias become, in fact, the main recipients of the practice of obligatory stay. With this rule, the State contributes, in fact, to spread mobsters and related interests in territories that until that moment had been hardly or at all characterized by an organized criminal presence. In Lombardy alone, for example, in the period considered, at least 400 men belonging to various clans arrive. The same also applies to other regions of Northern Italy starting from Piedmont, Emilia Romagna, Veneto and Liguria, up to design and rebuild the original criminal structures, making places of confinement of the original garrisons or first organized criminal cells. Consider that, despite of the ex governor of Lombardy and ex Ministry of the Interior, Maroni, in 2010 declared the non-existence of the mafias in that region[2], it was considered, already with the 2011 report of the Anti-Mafia Investigation Directorate (Dia), the fourth in Italy for properties seized from organized crime, after Sicily, Calabria and Campania, and second by number of offences concerning extortion (336), exceeded only by Campania (468). In Lombardy, the various mafia organizations, according to the investigators, would have divided the political management and some economic interests of many Municipalities and entered into agreements with the various foreign mafias: Rumanians, Albanians, Nigerians and Chinese in particular[3]. This dynamic "by law" is associated with the inclination of bosses and mobsters to widen the scope of their business and powers beyond the traditional

---

2   www.repubblica.it/politica/2010/11/16/news/maroni_saviano-9164864/
3   In the case of the province of Latina this concerns, in particular, the Indian crime dedicated to the international traffic of human beings for the purpose of labor exploitation (Omizzolo M., Carchedi F., 2016, "Il sistema criminale degli indiani punjabi in provincia di Latina", in Mafie straniere in Italia. Come operano, come si contrastano, by Stefano Beccucci, Francesco Carchedi, FrancoAngeli, Milan, p. 126-144).

geographic boundaries of the relative mafia organization. They sought new markets in the north of the country in an economic period in which money was legally and illegally circulated unreasonably. The economic boom, in fact, badly administered by the ruling class at that time, has facilitated the "internal migration" of numerous mobsters to settle and take root in the centres of economic and political power in Northern Italy. There is also a third reason that explains the process of mafia colonization in the north of the country, that is the substantial acceptance of the mafia of some northern entrepreneurs and politicians, also because of the large amount of money available to them. On the other hand, one of the first mobster identified in the North was Giuseppe Doto, called Joe Adonis, who ran gambling joints and night clubs in Milan. Finally, it should not be forgotten that in Milan, in 1970, a summit was held among the major bosses of the Sicilian Cupola, I.e. Totò Riina, Tommaso Buscetta, Gerlando Alberti and Gaetano Badalamenti[4]. These meetings are held only in places considered, from their point of view, completely safe or their property.

From the analysis carried out by the Central Operative Service of the State Police and by the Carabinieri of the Special Operational Grouping, it appears that the most important presence in the Lombard capital has always been the 'ndrangheta. It represents the mafia organization, also historically linked to the agricultural sector, more rooted in the north of the country and, in particular, in key sectors such as construction, waste traffic, public tenders and subcontracts affecting the health system, but also hotels , restaurants and drug traffickers to which, as will be seen, the conditioning of the relative fruit and vegetable market with the stable and established presence also in a judicial way, for example, of the dangerous Calabrian clan of Piromalli. Just this last aspect is one of the focus of this essay and reflect, among various ideas, to consider the mafias still agricultural traction, although able to expand and diversify their areas of interest in an extremely efficient. Dalla Chiesa with reference to the mafias in the North, he correctly states that "among the so-called non-traditional areas the greatest weight seems to have been played for several years by Lombardy, the richest and most eurospean region of the country. The reasons for the arrival and rooting of the mafia organizations in this region have been indicated in numerous studies and researches. Today it

---

4   The murder of the lawyer Giorgio Ambrosoli in 1979, liquidator of the Italian Private Bank, engaged in an important and dangerous action to combat the illicit operations desired by Michele Sindona and Roberto Calvi to favor the investments of the mafia gangs, still denotes, already at the end of the '70s, the advance of the mafias in the invisible but profitable market of finance.

is possible to trace these lines of tendency, which in some territories lead to creeping colonization processes: a force of systematic expansion in the fabric of medium and above all small municipalities, with the emergence (unspoken) of authentic emergencies, from Seregno to Rozzano a Tribiano; the establishment of a highly interwoven recycling economy with the legal economy, and a growing meeting of demand and supply of services and illegal goods between the white economy and the black economy; the establishment of two major centres of attraction: a major one consisting of the large conurbation of Milan-Brianza, the other minor consisting of Lake Garda; the advance from the south of the 'ndrangheta clans, towards the provinces of Mantua (in particular), of Cremona and of Lodi and Pavia (to an older settlement); a scientific and non-contrasted penetration in the public and private health sector; a progressive reduction in the areas of democracy and the frequent (and neglected) episodes of intimidation towards the opposition municipal councillors or associative exponents who are more committed to the rule of law; the entry into the scene, in no longer episodic form, of foreign organizations, with novelties of interest in the presence of Slavic-Balkan groups. At the same time, however, Lombardy has qualified in recent years both for a high capacity for contrast by the specialized structures of the State and for the development of one of the most important anti-mafia movements at the national level, branched out in schools, universities, in associationism, and also in the municipal administrations, as well as in a rich editorial and artistic production... In Piedmont organized crime is rooted because of a historical presence of the 'Ndrangheta and, to a lesser extent, of Cosa Nostra, to which they are alongside new organized criminal organizations, the so-called. foreign mafias, whose modus operandi, with reference to the Nigerian mafia and the Romanian one, was thought to be linked to that of the historical mafias. The most recent investigations point to a clear dominance of the 'ndrangheta, particularly rooted in the city of Turin and its province as well as in lower Piedmont and linked significantly with the Calabrian summits in the motherland, as well as other counterparts established in other regions. The investigations have highlighted the inclusion of the Calabrian organized crime both in the economic fabric (building and night clubs), and in the area of action of politics and public administration highlighting the close relationships existing with politics and the world of legal economy (see Albachiara survey) "(Dalla Chiesa N., 2017)[5].

5   Dalla Chiesa N., 2017, Mafie e Italia, www.giustizia.it/resources/cms/documents/
     Tavolo_5_Mafie_e_Italie.pdf

The Dia (Anti-Mafia Investigation Department), again with the report of the first half of 2011, affirms, with an extremely interesting reflection also from a sociological point of view, the methods for settling the various mafias in that region: "*the realization of the aims of the mafia associations it necessarily passes to the occupation of the territory and intimidation but to the practice of the approach / subjection (often conscious and consenting) of subjects linked in the same places by commonality of interests, as for example the building contractors operating in the area where the greater is the influence of the criminal group or, again, politicians and public administrators willing to sign pacts of connivance for an electoral or economic return*". A process that overcomes stereotypes and prejudices about the mobster modus operandi and that helps to explain the reasons why they can easily overcome the trauma of arrest and confiscation of their assets. In fact, they demonstrate an extraordinary resilience also in terms of practices and behaviours of settlement and rooting in various territories that are an expression of certainly sophisticated ways compared to the ancient practices of violence and direct intimidation alone. A sort of advanced mafia governance. These are structure that do not leave killed dead on the road, or at least only in extreme cases, but the fundamental rules and procedures of democracy. The report of Dia still refers to the existence of at least sixteen observed clans among Milan, Como, Brianza and Pavia. "Here in Lombardy we are five hundred men, Cecè; we are not just one", reports Saverio Minasi, head of the 'local' of Bresso, to Vincenzo Raccosta of the 'local' of Oppido Marmetina in Calabria. In the Municipalities of Buccinasco (called 'the Platì of the North') and Cernusco sul Naviglio the Calabrian historical gangs have settled: Talia, Bruzzaniti, Barbaro and Papalia, the latter then condemned at first instance for having conquered with intimidation the sector of the road transport. In Lecco there is the powerful clan of Coco Trovato, while in Monza the Mancuso, Iamonte, Arena and Mazzaferro clans stand out. In Varese, the domination belongs to the clan Farao Marincola of Catanzaro, while in Brescia and Bergamo (but also in Sondrio and Como) that one of the Bellocco of Reggio Calabria. Regarding Brescia and Bergamo, Dia reports:

"*Past investigations against people affiliated to the Calabrian ndrangheta present in Bergamo and Brescia, have shown that these subjects have referred to the thugs of the origin places to resolve the reciprocal disputes and to receive directives on the various activities to be carried out, not hesitating to associate with each other, depending on the different operational needs. In the presence of such groups, the phenomenon of extortion is linked to some commercial activities, in particular nightclubs and credit recoveries carried out relying on the intimidation force deriving from belonging to the southern crime. These criminal groups are also particularly active in the construction sector, where they also carry out the illegal work of intimidation (the Gang-masters), through which they manage to enter business activities and acquire the management of construction sites"*. Gang-masters (offence of illicit intimidation), therefore, activity certainly not unknown in this country (Omizzolo M., Sodano P., 2014)[6], and rooting capacity through its implicit intimidating force to the point of determining a sort of voluntary submission or subordination, sometimes by interest, by various subjects (freelancers and politicians) as well as companies and financial companies.

The Gang-masters, as an illegal recruitment activity, isn't absolutely extraneous, therefore, not even in those campaigns and farms. For example, the case of Rovigo can be cited where eighteen workers were employed, in 2017, without a regular contract in a farm in the district of Rovigo, Concadirame, through caporals. The workers, of Moroccan origin, were employed in the harvest fruits and vegetables. The employer, native of Polesine, was reported for exploitation of illegal immigration. In Grosseto, on the other hand, there would be over 3000 workers employed without a regular contract and more than half in the grape harvest. These data are reported by Fai Cisl that detects the employment of workers originally from Africa and Asia, who, after their activity in the countryside, work as street vendors on the beaches of Lazio and Campania. These person would work for a maximum of 40 euros a day (more often for 25-30) for 10-12 hours daily, which would result in the obligation to pay 5 euros per day for the corporal to transport to the workplace, 1.5 euros for a bottle of water, 3.50 euros for the meal and about 250 euros a month for the rent of housing, often crumbling. Tragic is the case of a Romanian worker who died in September 2016 at the age of 66 for a sudden illness while, with other fellow countrymen recruited by a Romanian cooperative, he was at work in a vineyard in Erbusco, in the district of Franciacorta. Finally, the police in the countryside of Asti, between August 21st and September 11th, 2016, controlled wineries in the Canelli and Nizza Monferrato territories in order to fight Gang-masters and exploitation of labor, discovering intermediation practices illicit, irregular employment of migrant labor, often regularly resident, and child labor. On November 6, 2018, the Pistoia police arrested three people accused of illegal brokering and exploitation of labor. The investigations revealed that the exploited workers were

---

6   Omizzolo M., Sodano P., 2014, Migranti e territori , Ediesse editor, Rome.

carried, without any precaution, on the boxes of four vans, all finished under seizure, covered by tarpaulins. The pay was four euros to work in the vineyards and olive groves of seven Tuscan provinces such as Pistoia, Siena, Prato, Florence, Lucca, Arezzo and Pisa. The searches also involved two commercial studies of Pistoia in use by a labor consultant who was in turn denounced.

The conditions that determine the labor exploitation in the countryside derive from the structural condition of necessity of the worker, from which the disequilibrium of its relationship of force towards the employer. They are not marginal or exceptional but central expression of a system of production and commercialization based on the instrumental and structural complicity of different subjects, such as the employer, the corporal, the trafficker, public subjects, freelancers, agro-industrial companies, governments, Large Organized Distribution and also exponents of various mobster clans (natives and foreigners) (Omizzolo M., 2016)[7]. It is this combination of subjects, each time different in relation to the historical-social, territorial, economic and political context, to determine a sort of real union aimed at obtaining profit and power, organized not in antithesis but in a structured way in the production system in force, reopening the need for a reflection on the merits of the characteristics of contemporary capitalism and its functional dynamics and logics.

According to the estimates of the report Agro-mafia and Gang-masters of the Flai-Cgil (2018), for example, only in Italy there would be about 400-430 thousand workers who daily suffer various forms of labor exploitation, of which about 80% are migrants. On the other hand, about 100 thousand workers in agriculture who live in conditions of serious labor exploitation with a varied intervention of about 26 mafia clans. In this point of view, 62% of migrant are seasonal workers employed in agriculture and do not have access to essential agricultural services, 64% do not have access to running water and 72% have, after the activity of harvest, diseases which earlier did not present (musculoskeletal diseases). In Italy there are also about 80 agricultural districts at risk where Gang-masters is a common practice; of these, 33 present "indecent" working conditions and 22 forms of serious work exploitation. The Gang-masters, moreover, is based on the misappropriation of part of the workers' salaries by the caporal: it can reach almost 50% of their income to reach a daily salary that varies between 25 euros and 30 euros, for an average 10-12 working hours. The caporals can also impose taxes that further burden workers' income: 5 euros for

---

7   Omizzolo M., *La Quinta Mafia* , RadiciFuture, Bari, 2016.

transport, 3.5 euros for sandwiches and 1.5 euros for each bottle of water consumed. The cost of the Gang-masters is also borne by the State in terms of tax damage: about 600 million euros are deducted each year from the tax authorities because of illegal brokering and tax evasion in a context where the underground economy in the agricultural sector is worth about 9 billion euros a year. Ultimately, productive, distributive and commercial chains are governed or conditioned by national and transnational organizations, including mafia, often based on illicit brokering of labor and on the international trade, the antechamber of exploitation and enslavement.

From a central point of view for the reflection proposed here, of the Gang-masters and the agro-mafias, we cite, to give an example, a brilliant operation conducted in July 2018 by the Financial Police of Pavia, which has arrested twelve people for the crimes of criminal association aimed at tax fraud, illegal brokering of labor (Gang-masters) and exploitation of labor taking advantage of the need of workers. In fact, it emerged that not only the wages paid were not in line with the provisions of national collective labor agreements but, in some cases, the workers were forced to return part of the salary received to the caporal. The forty cooperatives present in the logistics area were headed, through a series of corporate screens and a figurehead, to a single group of people, each with its own role within the criminal association, whose objective was to defraud the Treasury and exploit workers' needs. In fact, even though they worked and had a salary, they were willing to do shifts of twelve hours a day, without planning weekly rest periods, holidays or paid expectations. Furthermore, an evasion of value added tax for € 5.8 million and an omitted payment of social security contributions for € 9.2 million were ascertained. In addition to the arrests, the investigating judge has ordered the requisition of movable and immovable property for over 14 million euros executed in collaboration with the provincial commands of the Fiamme Gialle of Milan, Turin, Bergamo, Brescia, Lodi, Pescara, Aosta, Genoa, Catanzaro, Latina, Palermo, Rome and Naples. A similar situation was identified, among others, also in Mantua, for labourers employed for 12-13 hours of daily work for salaries that did not exceed three euros per hour, residing in crumbling or precarious housing such as campers and caravans, with a bathroom available for 25 people. This derives from a brilliant operation against the Gang-masters conducted by the Carabinieri of Mantua who arrested six people (one Italian and five Bangladeshi citizens), responsible for the crime of Gang-masters (art.199 of the c.p.).

Gang-masters, criminal affairs, agricultural and food supply chain, therefore, are an opportunity for mafias to realize millionaire businesses, to recycle money and to conquer strategic sectors for the country's democracy. Unacceptable are, from this point of view the thesis of the ex prefect of Milan, Gian Valerio Lombardo, who, in a hearing in the Parliamentary Commission about the organized crime, argued that in the main town of Lombardy there would be single mafia families but not the mafia, there are gangs but they are entrepreneurial more that criminals. The first family of 'ndrangheta to be known in Lombardy is that one of Giacomo Zagari, disavowing this thesis, originally from San Ferdinando, in the Gioia Tauro Plain, moved in 1954 first to Galliate Lombardo and then to Buguggiate (Varese). His son will become a key witness of the Isola Felice major trial, at the end of which seven life sentences and over 600 years in jail for 52 defendants were arranged.

Similar experiences have been identified in Piedmont, one of the most important economic realities in Italy and in Europe. This region boasts the sad record of hosting the first municipality dissolved by the Mafia. In 1995, in fact, the administration of the Municipality of Bardonecchia was dissolved because of the confined Rocco Lo Presti, living there starting from 1963 with the law of coerced stays. Bricklayer of Marina Gioiosa Jonica (Reggio Calabria), linked to Francesco, called Ciccio Mazzaferro, also confined in Valsusa (and investigated in 1976 for having obtained contracts for the Frejus tunnel), and then to the Ursino clan thanks to his sister's marriage with one of them. Lo Presti over time assumed the monopoly of several sectors (construction, trade with bars, restaurants and amusement arcades and, in this case too, to the road transport) bringing from Calabria to Val di Susa a considerable amount of labor often forced to work in conditions of serious labor exploitation: money laundering, rackets with low-priced workforce non-organised workers, loan-shark, intimidation, and, of course, infiltration into politics, according to the classic scheme of exchange for votes to gain favors, these are the absolute rule. Still, therefore, the non organised labor and employed in conditions of labor exploitation for the responsibility of the mafias[8]. In the period between the seventies and the

---

8   As a result of the courageous opposition of Mario Ceretto, a building contractor, who in 1975 refused to take on the work of Lo Presti, he was kidnapped and killed. For this reason Lo Presti was sentenced at first instance to 26 years in jail, locked up in the supermax prison of Asinara in the cell with Tommaso Buscetta, but acquitted in final appeal in 1982. Fourteen years later the arrest for mafia, linked to the scandal of Camp Smith, a mess of building contracts that fills with cement one of the oldest winter tourism resorts in Piedmont and which causes the dissolution of the municipality of Bardonecchia for the mafia. Following the investigation that ensues, the mayor, the municipal secretary, the town planning consultant and the planner are sentenced. The resurrected Lo Presti, sentenced

eighties, in Piedmont, there remained, finally, a period of high mobster density with 37 kidnappings in that region.

But what does all this have to do with agro-mafias, labor exploitation, Gang-masters? The relationship is direct and the welding is evident. The links among the mafias are strong and the business sectors are the terrain on which they compete, unite and clash. Lombardy and the mafia directly recalls, for example, the management of the Fruit and Vegetable Market of Milan, owned by the municipality through the company So.Ge. Mi (a company that manages the whole aerial of the whole fruit market on behalf of the Municipality), which has been the subject of at least twenty years of various journalistic investigations and numerous anti-mafia operations. The 2007 preventive detention order against Salvatore Morabito (exponents of the Morabito of Africo gang), Antonino Palamara, Pasquale Modaffarri and other 21 people, has put in evidence, for example, the infiltration and rooting of the Morabito-Bruzzantini gang, within the large and important Milan market, thanks to the recruitment of the entrepreneur Antonio Paolo, owner of the grouping of cooperatives Nuovo Co.Se.Li. In fact, it used the whole fruit market as a logistic point for the international traffic of cocaine, with a lot of night clubs, the For the King, opened in a place of the So.Ge.Mi., whose management was entrusted to SPAM, also based in the same building. This other criminal activity lasted from 2003-2004 until 2007. These companies consisted of five consortiums of cooperatives, which managed to obtain procurement

---

to six years in 2002 by mafia association, is again acquitted on appeal. A strange coincidence that finds similar oddities in many other procedural events of the Mafia in Italy. On 22nd January 2009 the definitive sentence, this time for usury: Lo Presti died the following day, a few hours after the transfer from the hospital of Orbassano to the prison ward of the Molinette of Turin. A similar fate of Ceretto belongs to the prosecutor Bruno Caccia, who was killed in Turin on 13 June 1983. The conspirator, 'ndranghetista Domenico Belfiore, who was sentenced to life imprisonment, declared that "with Caccia could not talk noone". The accuracy and intransigence of the judge contrasted the good relations that the Calabrians had managed to establish with some magistrates from Turin, with whom, obviously, the dialogue was much easier. The period between the eighties and nineties is also a period of many repentants, like Salvatore Parisi, known as Turinella, a leading figure of the Corsoti clan, captured in Turin on September 1984 just a few minutes after completing the last murder, the one of Domenico Carnazza. He will confess 21 murders, in addition to reconstructing other 40 and to make excellent names and surnames. His testimony will lead to the arrest in Milan of Angelo Epaminonda called 'O Tebano, successor of Francis Turatello and important boss of the Ambrosian crime, but will also unleash a megablitz with the arrest of a hundred people including men of the institutions.

contracts for millions of euros from public and private companies, over the whole fruit market, followed by subcontracts to second level cooperatives. Morabito's task was, according to the investigations, to organize the corporate structures, recruiting, among the trusted men of the group to which they belong, the directors of the companies operating within the hometown, acquiring the availability of nightclubs and meetings various members, logistical means, such as telephones and cars registered to employees or directors of companies. In this case, the money laundering operations were carried out through companies known as paper mills, which were responsible for issuing invoices for non-existent expenses in order to favour the distribution of profits among the various members of the gangs quantified in approximately nine million euros. The gangs and its multiple corporate structures had acquired, moreover, in addition to the use of the structures above, even the monopoly of internal activities such as porterage, cleaning, daily employment and access control. In 2004, Salvatore Morabito, returning from the period of coerced stays at Africo (Reggio Calabria), is honoured with a pass issued by So.Ge.Mi for his movements within the commercial area and to be able to enter with Ferrari of his property. Ferrari and champagne, but also fruit and vegetables produced in the Italian countryside through criminal and mobster systems of local and international recruitment that produce a business and political system (i.e. management of public power) that is intertwined with the legal system, marketed through distribution systems of national and international relief.

To update this criminal model, which has become habitual governance, it is useful to remember that in 2017 the Milan market was once again interested in an investigation ("Providence" operation) of the DDA of Reggio Calabria. The protagonists change, but the previous story is repeated. New is the reference clan, that one of the Piromalli in this case, the new leader (also members of allied gangs like Mazzaferro and Alvaro) Antonio Piromalli, regent of the clan, the old method of settlement inside the structure, as well as the connection with international trafficking of drugs. Underlines the DDA of Reggio Calabria that Antonio Piromalli, at least since 2014 had taken control of the MOF of Milan, through the creation of a complex network of companies and the help of a series of affiliates and supporters, leveraging the mafia method exercised by his person[9]. In this regard, he was also an occult member of the societies of

---

9   Increasingly, the mafia action is exercised without the consequence action but just to recognize the belonging by those who they want to subordinate. For this reason,

Ortopiazzolla and Polignanese, determining the commercial strategies of the same and advantaging of them in order to achieve ever greater illicit gains through the management of a commercial network for the marketing of clementine and oranges of Calabrian origin, then placed on the Italian mass distribution circuit, as well as in Romania, Denmark and other countries. The same subject provided for the financing of the mafia organization through recycling operations in business and commercial activities, after the concealment of the illicit origin of money. The combination of traffics of narcotic substances, considered among the collateral activities, is unmissable. Another criminal activity of Piromalli consisted in the management of a holding company made up of various companies (both under Italian and US law) active in the agri-food sector, with particular reference to the marketing and oil and citrus fruit export. In this way, not only the assets coming from illegal activities was reinvested, but large scale frauds were organized against the American consumers, producing a substantial money flow, however subtracted from taxation, through false invoices, use of credit cards, anonymous credit and payments abroad off the books.

All the different realities analysed, the result of the judicial operations that allowed the identification of mafia organizations active in the sector, show, therefore, the relevance of a dynamic phenomenon, in continuous evolution, which has ancient roots and which lives the control exercised on the territory and the advantages deriving from the management of mass distribution centres and fruit and vegetable markets.

No less significant, in this regard, is the case of the Fruit and Vegetable Market of Fondi (MOF), one of the largest in Italy and among the largest in Europe. The mafia infiltration regarding this important junction between the fruit and vegetable production of Central and Southern Italy and the large markets of the North and of Europe, took place by various mafia organizations and in particular by 'ndrangheta and camorra. In 2007 it was the District Anti-Mafia Direction (DDA) of Reggio Calabria to investigate two subjects, Carmelo and Venanzio Tripodo, living in the Municipality of Fondi (LT), coerced stays of their father Domenico Tripodo, one of the historical boss of the province of Reggio Calabria. The two controlled through intimidation made mainly against wholesalers of Calabria and Sicily, the access of the latter to the Fondi fruit and vegetable market. In particular, they forced numerous Sicilian and Calabrian entrepreneurs in

---

the exercise of mafia violence is only secondary and more and more exceptional while the concept of the mafia method becomes more articulated.

the sector to make permanent use of their intermediation to work in the field of shipments of goods from the agricultural centre of Vittoria[10] at the Fondi fruit and vegetable market, with the collaboration of exponents of organized criminality in the Sicilian city[11]. More recently, it was the turn of the DDA of Naples, with the operation "GEA" to determine the passage of dominion on that market to the Camorra and precisely to the Casalesi and the Mallardo. Among them there was a sort of pact of a real division of the fruit and vegetable business, in which the Casalesi managed the MOF and the Mallardo the Giugliano centres. Another family of Camorra – the one of D'Alterio – was in charge of achieving and maintaining the monopolistic management and control of road transport from and to the fruit and vegetable markets of Fondi, Aversa, Parete, Trentola Ducenta and Giugliano and from these markets to the South -Italy and in particular towards the Sicilian markets of Palermo, Catania, Vittoria, Gela and Marsala.[12]

---

10 As part of this reflection, we focus on the fruit and vegetable markets of Milan and Fondi. However, the Vittoria market, in Sicily, deserves to be examined further, because it is part of the same system. For further information on this issue, refer to the investigations and reflections by the journalist Paolo Borrometi and the magistrate Bruno Giordano.

11 According to the investigators, in a phone call admitted to the proceedings of the related trial Venanzio Tripodo has ordered the administrator of Mof spa, Giuseppe Addessi (still in charge with the same role): "In the Mof enters just who I want". It was the Commission of access to reconstruct in detail the ties between the brothers originating in Calabria and political exponents of the Municipality of the South Pontino:"... *the connections that emerged clearly during the access between the Tripodo family and those linked by parental appear highly significant, also to top figures of the Municipality of Fondi, as well as owners of commercial activities fully included in Mof*". On the other hand there were already established connections "*of the Tripodo family with elements of the Calabrian mafia and Camorra clans, in particular that one of the Casalesi*". The chain of relationships included Venanzio Antonino Tripodo (brother of Giovanni Carmelo) in very close relations with Franco Peppe, owner of the stand at Mof, who, being his cousin, was in close contact with the current mayor, Luigi Parisella, as well as with Aldo Trani who had direct relations with subjects of high crime and had benefited from a condescending behavior of the City of Fondi.

12 The presence of the mafias in the province of Latina, in particular the Casalesi clan, is sanctioned by the sentence issued following the procedure instructed by the DDA of Rome (so-called "the 1990s,") in which is recognised the existence in Castelforte (LT) of an autonomous criminal group but linked to the clan through Beneduce Alberto and Michele Zagaria. Likewise, the "Damascus 2" procedure, defined with a final ruling on September 4, 2014, has enshrined the establishment and operation of the Tripodi-Trani mafia clan, an association that has assumed "connotations" of mobsters in consideration of its stable and enduring operation

These are mobster entities that have seriously damaged the economy of the country, introducing destabilization factors in the food supply chain through the cancellation of the mechanisms of free competition, the exclusion of honest entrepreneurs from the food supply chain, also given their consequent difficulty in accessing to credit, the loss of attractiveness for EU or non-EU investors, the interference on the possibilities of creating new jobs, the spread of recycling activities and the connivance of public employees who have also contaminated and conditioned the action public administration.

Particular attention must be paid to the mechanisms of disbursement of community funds, often altered through false substitutive declarations or false documents attesting ownership of private or public land for non-titled subjects. To this end, the administrative control system should be strengthened and, in any case, replaced with respect to the current forecast, based on mere self-certification. The latter are not able to show the distortions present in the allocation procedures of the funds and often constitute the ideal coverage. The current legislation, although in many ways tested in the establishment of adequate networks to combat organized crime, still appears insufficient in the prevention of phenomena that often take on transnational dimensions thanks to increasingly complex agro-food supply chains. In fact, the use of these articulated structures is beneficial for exploiting their economic potential. In these contexts, the availability of some creditors to areas of local organized crime for the recovery of their credit due by defaulting debtors were recorded in areas subject to mafia control, with the obvious consciousness of the mafia, intimidation and violent method to which the debtors they would have been subjected.

II   In view of the importance that Italian agro-food plays at national level in guaranteeing the positive balance of the country's trade balance[13],

---

with intimidating methods, since the early 90s, in a territory like that one of Fondi,outside in the past, by geographical location, to events of organized crime and therefore more fragile and exposed for their infiltrating character, have assumed with time more and more carat and effectiveness, with the aim of committing an indefinite series of crimes (drug trafficking, weapons, usury, extortion) and to acquire control of internal economic activities thanks also with the support of external supporters".

13   In 2017, according to the ISMEA report "The national agri-food trade balance in 2017", overall exports of agri-food products exceeded the threshold of € 41 billion, up 6.8% on the previous year. This result is mainly attributable to the food industry, which accounts for 83% of agri-food exports and which showed an

in promoting a significant flow of exports and in sustaining income and employment, the Italian agri-food sector is a strategic source of lucrative trades that they end up harming the agricultural production system while it strengthens, instead, the agro-mafia chain and its complex of economic interests and relations. The Italian agricultural sector with its 1.2 million annual work units (Istat, 2017)[14] and about 1.6 million enterprises (ICE, 2017)[15] is one of the fundamental architraves of the entire Italian industrial system. In December 2016, Italy had the highest number of recognized food certifications (PDO, PGI and TSG) at EU level, with 291 top quality agri-food specialties and 83,695 certified operators (ISTAT, 2018)[16]. This is a business that in 2016 gave the country an added value of about 31.6 billion euros, with a relative weight on the EU-28 agri-food value added of 18.8%; an amount that puts Italy in first place in Europe (Istat, 2017)[17]. Not to mention that total exports are around € 38.4 billion (ICE, 2017), downstream of an industry that could reach € 190 billion, about 13.9% of GDP. Some important personalities speak, in this regard, as magistrate Caselli[18], of "liquid mafia" to indicate the capillary infiltration of the criminal economy in contexts that, originally oriented towards legality, are more and more often bent to the logic of malfeasance through the use of illicit tools that destabilize the market[19].

---

annual increase of 7.5%. Even the agricultural sector has recorded an increase in exports (+ 3.4%).

14   Istat, 2017, The trend of Agricultural Economy, year 2016, 19 may.
15   ICE (Agency for the promotion abroad and the internationalization of Italian companies), 2017, L'Agro-food in Italy, Production and Export.
16   Istat, 2018, Quality agro-food products DOP, IGP, STG, year 2016, 15 January.
17   Istat, 2017, Private household consumption, year 2016, 6 July.
18   Abstract of Giancarlo Caselli about "Agro-mafias" fot "General States of the Mafia Fight", 2017, tav. 16.
19   This is an evolution that has been discussed for many time. In this respect, care must be taken. The mafias expand territorially but do not renounce their historical territorial anchorage and their traditional vocations, starting from the control of the territory and from those sectors, such as agriculture, which are still the inspiration and objective of the mafias. Some academics have, in fact, supported, yielding to an excess of theoretical systematization, that "*international organized crime has globalised its activities for the same reasons as legitimate multinational companies*", so that the concepts of territorial rooting and control would be considered obsolete for what it is a global crime multinational which "*transcends the sovereignty that organizes the system of the modern state*", within the framework of a more general context of deterritorialisation of economic power. In reality, "*despite of the globalization and the theses that want the liquid and immaterial mafias, postmodern and*" in Internet ", the 'ndrangheta in the North continues to try to enter in a local market par excellence, that one of construction,

In this respect, even with all the necessary distinctions, some judicial investigations help to understand the dynamics of this phenomenon. For example, the operation conducted by the Forlì economic-financial police unit in September 2018 in Emilia Romagna is very interesting. In fact, it has found paid workers between 3 and 6 euros per hour with work shifts in the countryside of even 14 consecutive hours, sometimes even without food and water. This is why three men of 31, 33 and 34 years of Moroccan nationality, regularly in Italy and inhabitants in Verona, were arrested on charges of Gang-masters and use of illegal labor and two owners of three farms were investigated (two in Forlì and one in Cesena). The three entrepreneurs, in one of the richest and best organized regions also in terms of social services in Italy, are accused of having recruited and employed labor under exploitation conditions in agricultural companies in the province of Forlì-Cesena, Ravenna and Verona. The investigations were initiated following reports by the Financial Police on the basis of inspections of the Labor Inspectorate in August 2017. The three arrested persons also managed, through nominees, several cooperative societies with which they recruited dozens of workers to be allocated to agricultural enterprises operating above all in the chicken breeding sector. Injuries and illnesses entailed reproaches and serious penalties for the worker. Also disadvantaged housing conditions, characterized by overcrowding and lack of adequate sanitation. Other important operations deserve to be mentioned starting from the one that hit the Mafia of Gela, in Sicily, in particular the Rinzivillo clan and its business conducted in Rome, Northern Italy and Germany. Through inflated invoices, supplies of vegetables never ordered, prices higher than those agreed, the Sicilian bosses would have imposed themselves on the entrepreneurs of the Roman agri-food market of Guidonia, making it the centre of their agro-mobster business. It is a system discovered by the Rome and Caltanissetta prosecutors, coordinated

---

and continues to do in the same way he used to do in the Sixties". This also applies for the Sicilian Cupola, the Casalesi clan and even more for the different foreign mafias in the country. The history of the mafia is, therefore, in reality marked by a changeable synthesis between the control of the territory and the creation of partnerships with the external economic reality, between *"the territorial structure of the gangs with the rigid affiliations, the formidable continuity over time, military strength and therefore the ability to exercise, starting from the guardian mechanism, a vicarious function of public security – and the business network, necessarily comprising affiliates and non-affiliates"*. The relationship between these two spheres is not definable once and for all, but it varies according to the different historical and social contexts as well as from the ruling class to the government of the country and its institutions.

by the National Anti-Mafia and Antiterrorism Prosecutor's Office, which led to the precautionary custody of 37 people and the seizure of assets and companies for over 11 million euros. In Germany, Cologne and Karlsruhe, Rinzivillo activated a criminal cell thanks to contacts with the fugitive of 'ndrangheta Antonio Strangio, owner of the restaurant "Da Bruno" where in 2007 the massacre of Duisburg took place.

According to the ex-director of the Anti-Mafia Investigation Directorate and ex General of the Carabinieri, Girone, Mafia, Camorra and 'Ndrangheta would have come to the point of making agreements for the control of the agri-food sector throughout the country. Fondi, for example and once again, was the subject of the Sud Pontino operation[20]: *"I Casalesi – says General Girone – had imposed their presence on this market that is a true strategic hub of distribution. To this they added a check also on the regions of origin of the goods"*. This was possible with the construction of a mafia-'ndragheta-camorra sign that has brought paradoxical effects: *"For example, it happens that pachino tomatoes produced in Ragusa are brought to Fondi, here packaged and sent back to Ragusa to be sold"*. Taking into account that in this market the Casalesi *"imposed the protection money on every commodity"*, the effect on prices was direct. *"We are faced with surcharges ranging from 70% of the short chain, from the producer to the consumer, to 103% with only one intermediary, to 300% with the long chain. The paradox is that those who earn less in this system have been the producers"*. The former director of Dia points out that entry into the markets has occurred before with the establishment of companies to obtain public funding, then imposing the price and the protection money in a kind of criminal monopoly in which everyone has their own skills. *"In Fondi the Camorra organizations have joined the Calabrian families and mafia gangs, allowing, for example, that the Casalesi could operate on the market of Gela thanks to the involvement of even members of the family of Totò Riina – says the general. "The phenomenon clearly facilitates the emergence of illegal work, frauds against INPS and the European Community"*. And again Girone: *"It also affects the trafficking of illegal immigrants, who are under-employed in agriculture, giving rise to the hiring"*.

Just the investigative action has allowed, among others, to seize, through the provision of the prevention measures of the court of Trapani,

---

20   To know the origin and operational modality of the relationship contract between the different mafia organizations operating in the Pontino, we recommend "La Quinta Mafia" (Omizzolo M., RadiciFuture ed., 2016).

assets for 1 million and 800 thousand euros to Carmelo Cagliano, 50 years of Marsala, considered a nominee by the Anti-Mafia Investigation Directorate. Capital accumulated thanks to the almost absolute domination of the fruit and vegetable transport system. To reconstruct the story is the note of the anti-mafia investigative directorate: *"Free from convictions for mafia facts, the inclusion of Carmelo Gagliano in the underworld and the adherence to mafia logic of management of economic initiatives are linked to his role as administrator (as a nominee) of the Autofrigo Marsala in which the Mafia exponent of Marsala Ignazio Miceli was boasting. Thus emerged – continues the note – the existence, within the Mof, of a division of business by the criminal organizations and a monopolization of the road transport sector of the Casalesi clan".* The latter, in order to win exclusive control over the routes to and from Sicily, according to the investigations had formed an alliance with entrepreneurial emissaries of Cosa Nostra belonging to the Riina brothers. A key sector for the country that continues, despite of the important interventions of law enforcement and judiciary, to remain largely in the hands of mobsters and criminals. The relationship, however, between this system and labor exploitation in the Pontine countryside is direct. The mafias, in fact, crush rights and blow up the value of legal contracts. The consequences are paid by the weakest, the least organized, the most fragile and among these, in particular, in this case, the Indian labourers of the province of Latina[21].

From the availability of European funding flows, therefore, to the money laundering also through the use of the online network, including the practices of usury and extortion, the mafias see multiply their sectors of economic interest. On the other hand, precisely the last report of the Parliamentary Anti-Mafia Commission (XVII legislature) states that *"the progressive reduction of the violent and military components of the mafia method is recorded as a constant and consolidated element in all the territories and in all the organizations. They give way to the promotion of relations of exchange and collusion in illegal and even more legal markets. The identification of the conduct attributable to the mafia organizations, as such dangerous and deserving of adequate sanctioning response, therefore becomes more complex and involves a reexamination of the descriptive tools of illicit behaviour. But even more this evolution imposes a rethinking of anti-mafia policies aimed more at "context factors", that is the political,*

---

21   We invite you to visit the coop. site for further details In Migrazione (www. inmigrazione.it) and the one of the Tempi Moderni study centre (www.tempi-moderni.net).

social and economic conditions that favour the genesis and reproduction of the mafias, in a scenario in which the intertwining Mafia crime, corruption, economic crime and white-collar crime" (Final report of the Parliamentary Anti-Mafia Commission, 2018, page 14).

Ultimately, the activities of Law Enforcement and Judiciary unveil the presence of very complex mafias that are not content to resort to intimidation, as an instrument of original and therefore traditional action, but aspire to actively participate in economic life and social life of the country without taking overpowering and directly violent attitudes. In fact, they are generally rather subdued, apparently, in order to act in an undisturbed way, avoiding to trigger inspection and repressive activities by the police and the Judiciary. This is increasingly evident with reference to some extortion activities or illegal labor recruitment, carried out within a framework in itself mafia but without being expressed through violent actions. In fact, every public action put in place, turns on media spotlights and the attention of investigators and the media, which end up disturbing their social organization and the complex of economic interests that they manage to govern. For this reason, silent mafias respond to an evolved governance of their reference universe and are more suitable for achieving their goals. This, moreover, allows the strengthening of the still too widespread negotiating theses with respect to their role and economic-political power.

In the agri-food chain, the mafias, therefore, are awarded the control of sectors, prices, gestures, transport and distribution, exported the Made in Italy, they manage, often in alliance with some foreign mafias, the activity of illegal recruitment of labor to be used in the related knowledge, the participation of human beings for the purpose of labor and sexual exploitation and finally participate in the production of Italian sounding. This is an activity that can be defeated due to a series of laws of the rule of rights and the repression of the Mafia prejudice in support of the recent law against Gang-masters (199/2016) and of the Anti-Mafia Code.

The evolution of the phenomenon, inside which the scourge of Gang-masters and of the international treaty is also a purpose of labor exploitation, calls, in fact, a clear legislative response to prevent its diffusion from the qualification expressed by the new figure of agro-industry elaborated in the scope of the work of Caselli Commission about the reform of crimes in the agri-food sector. Following a reform of the complex of social services, which pursue a territorial level, must be able to intervene, with maximum professionalism, in places of hardship and to act on the needs of the phenomenon and emerging from only administrative approaches. The provision of specific capital measures must, moreover, be accompanied by more suitable solutions to valorize the confiscated assets, ensuring new life to economic activities weakened by the seizure procedures. The social and employment value of a seized, confiscated agricultural asset and, finally, an entrepreneurial project assigned a strong social vocation, not only an effective strategy to fight mafia but an extraordinary occasion to demonstrate the effectiveness of the state action also in responding legitimate requests for legality and regeneration of mafia assets, also in terms of employment, which emerge from the Italian population. The seizure and confiscation of a farm for mafia activity or for a Gang-masters must, in fact, become an occasion for rehabilitation of the same and its production chain, real protection for workers employed and for the territory. Too often, however, we witness seized companies and do not value adequate. They end up crystallizing in a limited administrative area, to which is added the unacceptable loss of jobs, due to economic crisis for their families and the territory. The challenge against the agro-mafia is easier to win, in fact, the country is a redevelopment of the areas and companies by the mafia and not a mortify for incapacity, default, lack of professionalism, wrong economic investment or even a cause of various forms of speculations about these resources. More structured and exposed is the supply chain and easier for successful companies in the economic structure, through the insertion of nominees in the corporate structure, the development of the aid system envisaged at European and national level, the nationalization of fruit and vegetables imported from foreign or, again, the application of usurious interests to operators who find themselves in illegal credit circuits, up to the use of some farms by the mafias such as big money-laundering, betraying their vocation and often acting with illicit advantages on the international, national and international market. In the analysis sector, the mafias show their interest in the sector of the entire production chain – starting from the ownership of considerable plots of land up to the retail sale of agricultural products – and in the control of the phases of the transport of goods, of the fruit and vegetable markets, as we have seen, and of the meat or of the catering activities.

With specific regard to the different matrices of the mafias present on the national territory, it is possible to distinguish the methods of infiltration, also detecting the individual points of contact. For example, Cosa Nostra in Catania is more involved in the management, directly or by means of nominees, of companies operating in the fruit and vegetable sector, in particular, in the citrus sector. These companies appear to be led by mafia methods, through the imposition of their products in large retail outlets, the impediment of the sale of other products, the imposition of the choice of the road transport agency of the products and, again, the impediment of road hauliers to carry out travel orders without their consent. These are criminal modalities that, among other things, prevent a correct entrepreneurial and occupational development of the area. Another sector infiltrated by the association is that one of meat intended as mass distribution circuit. Moreover, these are national and international commercial circuits and therefore capable of involving a large group of people and countries. For Cosa Nostra in Trapani are also recorded activities conducted in the olive market through the hidden management of oil mills and the management of agricultural land used for vineyards and citrus groves as well as through the undue perception of substantial EU contributions FEAGA (European Agricultural Fund Guarantee) obtained by concealing the effective ownership of the land.

Although not in Trapani but in Palermo, it deserves to be cited the operation of law enforcement conducted against the boss dell'Acquasanta who would have monopolized the sale of products and prices in some stands of the fruit and vegetable market in Palermo as well as the porterage and parking facilities, through a local cooperative. This is an investigation that began in 2014 and that led, in 2018, to the confiscation of an assets of about 150 million euros against Angelo and Giuseppe Ingrassia, both 61-year-olds, from Palermo, considered close to Cosa Nostra. Numerous real estate passes permanently to the State, i.e. buildings, apartments in Palermo, Ficarazzi and villas in Villagrazia di Carini, land, shops in the historic centre of the main town and warehouses, shareholdings in companies that deal with construction, trucks, cars and motorcycles and various banking relationships and financial products.

The Camorra clans, as already described, are mainly active in the fresh fruit and vegetable market, coming to control the largest wholesale centre located in Fondi (LT) and to acquire a monopolistic management of the road transport of products, imposing with force its carriers and profiting from the costs of transferring goods. Proceeds from illicit activities are reused in the purchase of commercial restaurants in Naples and other Italian cities.

The 'ndrangheta, however, through the activity of the hegemonic families in the province of Reggio Calabria, has spread through a tight control on economic activities in the fish, citrus and transport sectors, committing crimes to achieve illegal EU funding. Other ROS investigations have identified mafia organizations active in the control of wholesale and retail distribution of fruit and vegetables and food products sold to tourist accommodation in Vibo coast or active in the distribution of roasted coffee and derived products, bakery products and other foodstuffs, by expelling competing suppliers from controlled territory through acts of intimidation. This is a typically 'ndranghetist methodology that, through intimidation and threatened, feared or real, manages to conquer growing commercial and business sectors. The chestnut and grape to be squeezed sectors have also been the focus of the 'ndrangheta through the imposition of prices lower than half of the normal market price. Through the control of the consortia of companies in the province of Reggio Calabria, the criminal organizations have ensured the availability of supply of necessary and sufficient products to feed the chain of large retailers in the north-east of Italy as well as the Romanian market. Moreover, they have succeeded in carrying out illegal activities harmful to the image of Made in Italy through the export of oil to the United States and labelling the pomace oil as extra virgin olive oil. This is the clear demonstration of the ability of the mafias to condition sectors that are an expression of Made in Italy and which should be protected in a very efficient manner. The organized crime in Puglia – especially that one in the province of Foggia – has, finally, exploited the wine-growing campaigns to achieve undue perceptions to the detriment of the state and the European Union.

III The mass distribution circuit (abbreviated Gdo) has some characteristics that contribute to making it particularly attractive to individuals directly or indirectly linked to different mafia clans. For example, it manages numerous commercial activities in the form of retail sales of food products and non-food products in large-scale retail outlets distributed throughout the national territory. Because of this specific feature, which combines the aggregation of retail businesses within a nationwide territorial spectrum, the GDO is, for example, suitable for money laundering of illicit origin.

Another of its distinctive elements concerns the operation of sales points through "commercial chains" characterized by a single brand, around which promotional and commercial strategies are deployed to conquer increasingly large sectors of the relevant market. However, it uses large surfaces, with a minimum dimensional threshold. The corporate aggregates that make up the Gdo's commercial chains are, in fact, made up of shopping centres, mall, factories, outlet centres, discount chains, and so on. Examples of these chains are the centres Auchan, Carrefour, Lidl, Coop, Esselunga,

Billa, Panorama, and many other national and international commercial realities[22].

The advantages of unification of distribution under a single coordination and administration are different starting from the presence of economies of scale, the control of promotional strategies, the possibility of more favourable rental conditions, the common management of environments, pricing policies, the implementation of commercial policies and advertising campaigns, procurement (choice of suppliers and management of purchases). In general there is a distinction between mass distribution circuit and mass international distribution companies that manage points of sale, and organized distribution with retailers that consortium for certain activities such as purchases, commercial promotions, and so on. The GDO develops a business of several hundred million euros nationally and internationally. According to the latest study by Mediobanca on Gdo[23], in fact, in 2016 it would have invoiced millions of euros. The first group for turnover is Coop, followed by the Conad group, while the first for performance is Esselunga, which manages to register the record figure of 16 thousand euros in sales per square meter. Then there are the discounters, led by Lidl and Eurospin and the French giants (Carrefour and Auchan). Again in 2016, again according to the latest report of the Mediobanca study area, the turnover of the major Italian GDO operators would have grown by 1.9% in the last year. These are particularly important turnovers that become appealing for the mafias that have managed to penetrate, as we will see, until they assume, in some territories, not only in the South, the guide of local Gdo.

The relationship between the mafia and Gdo is confirmed by some important judicial inquiries in 2017 which once again highlighted how their priority objective, although not exclusive, consists in the laundering of money deriving from their multiple illicit activities. To achieve this goal, the GDO, with its long supply chain and the multiplicity of subjects that characterize it, constitutes a strategic sector. The mafias, in fact, are able to

---

22 In Italy the first example of GDO was made in 1957 in Milan by the Italian Supermarkets (first of all Esselunga then Billa), but the Italian brands of GDO have reached a lesser diffusion than foreign ones. The most common brands are Coop, Esselunga, Panorama. The judgment about this sales methods concentrated in large areas is not unequivocal. The GDO, in fact, causes a crowding-out effect towards small firms that are not able to sustain price competition, resulting, consequently, a depersonalization effect in neighbourhoods where shops cease to operate and a sense of extraneousness among consumers.

23 Mediobanca, The major italian (2011-2015) and international (2014-2015) groups of the Gdo food, Area Studi Mediobanca, 2016.

settle even in commercial activities and territories far removed from their places of origin. As highlighted by the DIA (2013), *"the most remarkable aspect of mafia phenomenology is the accentuated tendency to pollute the legal economy, where the mafia enterprises (...) break with an availability of resources that, in the current glimpse, characterized from a systemic economic crisis, makes them unbeatable competitors"*[24]. In the Northern Italian regions, the criminal phenomenon seems to present a different appearance compared to Southern Italy. This is linked to some specific process and to the characteristics of the territory to be infiltrated. In the first instance, in fact, the mafia contagion takes place largely through the equity market, thanks to which important amounts of money of illicit origin reach the companies creating mechanisms of dependence and conditioning[25].

This is a dynamic that must be implemented to at least two conditions: the presence of a mafia cell able to monitor their investment and to understand the characteristics of the territory in which it resides, and the collaboration of some freelancers able to clean up the illicit money correctly and not improvised and hide this practice in the folds of the formal and current regulations.

In this regard, it is worth mentioning, in 2017, the president of the Court of Appeal of Trieste, Oliviero Drigani, according to whom, with regard to infiltration and rooting of mafias in the north of the country, Friuli Venezia Giulia *"can constitute the fertile ground for the rooting of forms of organized illegality "because" even if it can not be included among the regions characterized by a strong and consolidated presence of criminal organizations exercising obvious forms of control of the territory, it nevertheless presents undoubted attractions for the interests of the*

---

24   Anti-Mafia Investigation Directorate, Report to the Minister of the Interior in Parliament. Activities carried out and results achieved by the Anti-Mafia Investigation Division, 1st semester 2013, p. 265.

25   The colonization by various mafia gangs of some Italian productive sectors, in the case of the primary sector to which the distributive-commercial one accompanies, has seen strategies of aggression evolved by the mafias aimed at settling and taking root even in the most developed regions of the country, where the largest number of healthy and renowned internationally companies are concentrated. In the North of Italy, the mafias, for example, have succeeded in altering the economic dynamics through the control of traditional sectors (a case in point are the public tenders) and the employment of new and diversified sectors, such as large-scale distribution, waste disposal, healthcare, online gambling, catering, counterfeiting, flora-nursery products and alternative and renewable energies. These are issues that have been studied and analyzed by Eurispes for many years with research documents and reports.

delinquent also organized and therefore it can not be considered immune to illicit phenomena connected to crime". In 2017, in fact, there were worrying cases in the Friuli Venezia Giulia region, with reference to the contracts and subcontracts of Fincantieri, to money laundering and to the catering sector with particular reference, as recognized by the same Court of Appeal, to a well-known group of regional pizzerias. Even Veneto, one of the richest regions of Italy, is still, according to the report of the DIA of 2017, territory in which criminal interests are rooted in some of the most important and organized mafia clans in Italy. "As emerged over the years – states the Court of Appeal – from the outcomes of various judicial police activities, in the Veneto there were presences of subjects linked to Cosa Nostra, which would tend primarily to take root economically on the territory with a stable presence, but not such to assume the connotations typical of the origin Region. The main purpose of these partnerships is, in fact, identified in the recycling and reinvestment of illicit capital, also through the acquisition of commercial and business activities, exploiting, if necessary, the work of local delinquent groups. Added to this is the strong availability of liquidity, which pushes the organization to replace the legal credit system and to practice usury". The various operations of the Carabinieri operated against the Piromalli family, as already seen, showed, once again, how much Veneto is a desirable area for organized crime. The Calabrian clan was able, in fact, to affect the Fruit and vegetable market of Milan and, through a dense network of companies related to it, to ensure the distribution of fruit in Veneto and Friuli, getting to market their products in the commercial chain of Gdo. Furthermore, Piromalli was the head of the Sunkist Italia company, specialized in the distribution of effervescent drinks and the same name of the American multinational Sunkist Ltd which, according to the documentation of the case, seems to have never been aware of the existence of what appeared to be important Italian branch.

In the same building where many companies belonging to different clans engaged in the GDO had their registered office, Sical Fruit srl was also located, due to a boss of the 'ndrangheta, Leo Talia, who also traded large quantities of heroin and cocaine. Also in the field of drug trafficking, Ipergela Lombarda Srl operated, also located in the area of the Milan Motor Market and fictitiously engaged in commercial activities.

In the order of the Prosecutor that led to the arrest of more than thirty people, the investigators spoke of "affiliates", "supporters" and the use of "mafia methods". A similar situation has been found with reference to the 'ndrangheta which, again according to the Court of Appeal "in particular the ones of Catanzaro and Reggio, although not rooted in the North-East of the country, continues to bring out clear signs of operations, especially in Veneto. In fact, there have been qualified presences of subjects' of ndrangheta on Padua, in the west of Verona and in the lower Vicenza, due to criminal aggregates of Cutro, Delianova, Filadelfia and Africo Nuovo. These events would have become obvious with reference, as well as to drug trafficking, also to catering, tourism and construction". The process of inclusion of the clan in the chain of large-scale distribution continues, therefore, even throughout the year 2017, becoming systematically more sophisticated, thanks to the help of high-level professionals, in particular lawyers and accountants.

The penetration of the mafias in the GDO has not economized even the largest and most famous corporate groups in the world. The Catanese clan of the Laudani, for example, would have succeeded, according to investigations still underway by the competent prosecutor, to penetrate even within the international giant Lidl, until obtaining millionaires for the restructuring of dozens of sale points, thanks to 'support of two unsuspected Milanese entrepreneurs.

In the operation conducted by law enforcement, close relations would emerge between some executives of the companies involved, often placed in judicial administration, and some personalities considered to belong to the Laudani family. In the conclusions of the provision with which the Measures for Prevention of the Court of Milan ordered the judicial administration of Lidl Italia Spa, it is declared that "in relation to the directions in which the mafia infiltration took place", a position of good faith of the leaders of the four directorates general Lidl of Volpiano, Biandrate, Somaglia and Misterbianco, at the centre of the investigation of the Milanese DDA, as "not only receive money to assign jobs in favour of the suspects (...) but entertain, in direct or indirect (this is not known) relations with subjects belonging to the mafia family of Laudani able to guide the choices "of the chain of GDO in assigning service contracts. In this case, the deputy prosecutor of Milan, Ilda Boccassini, head of the Milanese DDA, explained that the investigations concerning Lidl have ascertained that "they knew who to bribe, which were the right people to bribe. For those who wanted to corrupt – he reported – it was like fishing in a safe pond: they knew exactly who, how and where to find the people to be bribed. The whole investigation – he added – was conducted in full synergy with the judicial authority of Catania". In the precautionary order we read that the alleged criminal association would have obtained "contracts and service contracts in Sicily" from Lidl Italia and eurospin Italia through "donations of money to members of the Laudani family", mafia clan "able to guarantee the monopoly of these orders and the co-management of the works in Sicily". The arrested, moreover, would have obtained jobs from Lidl Italia in Piedmont through "corruptive dations". The same GIP, Giulio Fanales, writes of "stable enslavement of managers of Lidl Italy, responsible for awarding contracts, in order to obtain the assignment of orders, in favour of companies controlled by the members, in disregard of the rules of competition and with serious damage to the assets of the contracting company". In the intercepted conversations, the inquisitorial entrepreneurs refer to the "gifts to be given for the Christmas holidays to the various managers" of Lidl in order "to favour the acquisition of the works". They would have divided "the importance of the gift according to the function covered by the subject within the managerial framework". In an environmental interception of December 19, 2016 and reported in the provision, the two entrepreneurs "speak clearly of the important gift to be given to Tomasella," head of the warehouse in Volpiano, in the province of Turin, and of what to do to Simone Suriano (Lidl manager, finished under house arrest). With regard to the latter, Politi intends to *"prepare not a basket but only a package, since they already subsidize it with 4,000 euros per month"*. The Lidl Italia company, however, is not investigated and declares itself "completely unrelated to what was spread on May 15 by the main media in relation to the operation managed by the DDA". The company adds that it became aware of the affair on 15 May 2017 by the investigating bodies, making itself immediately available to the competent authorities, in order to facilitate investigations and clarify as soon as possible.

The Italian judicial chronicle also reports on small entrepreneurs who started their business by opening a single store and then find themselves, within a few years and thanks to massive investments of illicit capital coming from the mafias, leading national commercial empires and beyond. This target had been pursued, for example, by Giuseppe Grigoli, one of the managers of a well-known brand of Italian GDO and present, in particular, in western Sicily, already convicted with a final ruling for 416 bis. Grigoli is considered one of the most important and influential mafia leaders, so much that he considers him to the level of Matteo Messina Denaro, that is the most famous mafia boss still in hiding.

The organizational model found by the judicial authority of Grigoli with reference to the 6GDO group at the time of the seizure was anomalous compared to those commonly adopted. The activity of the 6GDO Group envisaged the supply of various types of goods in favour of sales outlets owned by the group but which would have been leased to third parties. Through this model, in the course of about ten years, the 6GDO Group has experienced a very rapid growth, reaching a turnover of around 90 million euros and the purchase of 10% of Despar Italia (owner of the right of use on the Italian market of the Despar brand)[26]. At the time of the seizure, the Group owned 48 supermarkets, many of which were leased to third parties, and employed a total of about 500 workers, with an estimated real estate portfolio of around 53 million euros. The growth of the company has seen its culmination with the construction of the Belicittà shopping centre, located in Castelvetrano, in the province of Trapani, whose property was, also in this case, Grigoli Distribuzioni Srl, 40% owned by the 6GDO Group, while the remaining shares were owned by Giuseppe Grigoli and his wife[27]. The Grigoli Group also includes other companies in the supply chain and small businesses specialized in the production of food products distributed through the Group's sales points. These included companies producing, processing, storing and selling food products such as oil, dairy products, fresh fruit and vegetables, meat and bakery products.

The 6GDO Group, in essence, "carried out above all an activity similar to those of pure logistics (purchase and delivery of goods), not directly managing any of the supermarkets. The management of the commercial network entrusted to third parties certainly envisaged a considerable risk assumption, since in the sector in question the direct control of the internal dynamics of the stores was of fundamental importance both from a commercial and financial point of view through the immediate availability of receipts. The direct consequence of this management structure was the lack of control of the incoming financial flows that were conditional on the will of the individual managers of the points of sale and remittances that periodically made the same to payment of the supplies and rents of the business unit. It should be noted that the establishment of the commercial network found at the time of the seizure it had been handled directly by Mr. Grigoli Giuseppe on the basis of fiduciary criteria, which had sold the business branch rent the sale points and made the consequent supplies without requiring the issue of special guarantees. It should be noted also that the failure to pay the supplies of one of the client managers, according to the documentation found in the haunt of the boss Bernardo

---

26   Also thanks to its particular corporate configuration, from the legal point of view, the SPAR, which is owned by the Despar brand, as well as the Despar Italia, have been able to declare extraneous to all the events related to 6GDO.

27   Until then employed as a housewife, Mrs. Grigoli suddenly found herself in charge, as sole director, of a company with about 100 million euros in turnover.

Provenzano, originates the criminal proceedings that led to the confiscation of the company "(Ribolla N., Notes for the Parliamentary Anti-Mafia Commission, Palermo, 03 March 2014 – Unpublished document).

As evident with the affair of the 6GDO group, the mafias are able to impose themselves in this sector through affiliates, intermediaries and nominees, recognized by the community as material executors of the will of the bosses; in virtue of the solidity of the mafia organization on the territory, a binding relationship of trust between entrepreneurs, customers and suppliers is determined. According to one of the numerous interceptions carried out against the defendants of the 6GDO group, the mafia recruitment assumptions of various employees, such as operators, workers, cashiers but also directors and administrative staff, was a prerequisite for the realization of the mafia project. "It was not just the clerks and cashiers: even the managers of the stores, as mentioned – we read in an interception – were" mafia "(...) In the province of Trapani alone, there were relatives of mafia families in 11 supermarkets on 40: the daughter of the killer VM, the son-in-law of the mafia boss TM, the cousin of the mafia boss of Marsala NB (...)"[28].

In the case of 6GDO, the management of labor by the gangs not only determines the labor supply prices that do not conform to those of the market, but also encourages forms of exploitation and illegal work. The violation of workers' rights and, more generally, of current regulations, is one of the peculiarities that characterize companies infiltrated by mafias. In this case clearly emerge the typical ways through which the mafia domain is developed in the logistics and retail sector[29].

This is a process that starts from the presence of distributors and / or sale points with positions of domination and monopoly, the imposition of products to the exclusion of others in stores[30] accredited by the mafias, controlled sales points, billing not aligned with benchmarking, turnover concentrations in particular areas of the company, definition of abnormal

---

28   Rizzo M., Supermarket Mafia, RX, p. 80.
29   It remains fundamental the information gathered with La Paganese process concerning the Mafia affairs organized in the Fruit and Vegetable Market of Fondi with reference, in particular, to the Corleonesi clan (with Gaetano Riina), the 'ndrangheta (Tripodo clan) and the Casalesi (Schiavone clan).
30   "In the northern area of Naples, the Nuvoletta family guaranteed that only certain food products, including Parmalat milk and Bauli panettone, were present on supermarket shelves. The big northern multinationals like Parmalat and Cirio agreed to come into contact with the Camorra in exchange for a near-monopoly. When the police discover these agreements, the companies declared themselves to be victims of the racket "(Varese F., Mafie in movimento, Einaudi, 2011).

discount plans, use of buildings of dubious ownership, use of intermediaries and agents, improper use of the brand, sale of counterfeit products and, finally, the use of the logo to acquire reputation and market and screen companies for the realization of illicit trafficking of various kinds.

In relation to the corporate function relating to the sale and distribution within the Gdo, it is useful to analyze another emblematic case such as that one of TNT, in which some of its employees are imputed, in the related process, to have constituted in Lombardy a ' ndrangheta, obtaining illicit profits through the management "of cooperating contractors of TNT transport services, financed in whole or in part with the price, the product or the profit of crimes". The mafia infiltration of TNT activities takes place, in fact, through the acquisition of the services distributed by the multinational by cooperating cooperatives controlled by the mafia, such as, for example, Autotrasporti Alma srl, Edilscavi srl, MFM Group srl and Coop Regina.

Another case concerns a chain of hard discounters, whose ownership would be due to Giovan Battista Giacalone, considered a business partner of Salvatore Lo Piccolo, the boss of San Lorenzo. Giacalone, already convicted of a mafia association, for years has been considered in Sicily the owner of a chain of hard discounters under the "Mio" sign that used as a logistics base for his business, including money laundering of illicit origin. In Palermo Paolo Sgroi, now deceased, was also employed in the same sector, and a supermarket chain under the "Sisa" trademark was seized by the competent Public Prosecutor's office, in whose management he was once again responsible for the inconvenient presence of Salvatore Lo Piccolo. In a "notes" with his signature, found in the den of Bernardo Provenzano, in Montagna dei Cavalli, the boss of San Lorenzo explained that it would be activated to find a job to a relative of the godfather in the supermarkets of Sgroi.

Among the various mafias involved in the GDO, the 'ndrangheta is perhaps the one that boasts the longest tradition characterized by small and large supermarkets directly managed by affiliates or nominees, along with the supply of goods and services and the recruitment of staff. In fact, these are commercial activities that tend not to suffer from economic crises or are less exposed to the volatility that characterizes other economic sectors, guaranteeing continuous profit margins over time and a constant flow of cash. The investigations merged in the procedure n. 4614/2006/21 RGNR DDA (so-called System-Absinthe), have offered elements of great interest that can detect the rise of two entrepreneurs close to the main gangs of 'ndrangheta. The investigations also ascertained the structuring of cartels of suppliers, an expression of the main mafia consortia, up to rebuilding a system of mafia power that conditioned the GDO.

The consolidated relationships that formed the backbone of the relationships between large-scale retailers and suppliers, were the basis on which the employee assumptions were inserted and the inclusion of economic flows probably of illicit origin, guaranteeing the interests of the 'ndrangheta in the field.

To understand the strategic importance of the Gdo for the 'Ndrangheta, it must be considered that the entrepreneurs arrested, following the failure of the GDM S.p.a. (for years one of the main Calabrian commercial chains with the "Quiper" brand), they represented the most important (for turnover and number of sales points) the Gdo group in the city of Reggio Calabria where they operated under the "Simply" brand, after the same Suraci, together with other members, had managed, always on behalf of the 'ndrangheta, first the supermarkets under the brand name "Vally Calabria" and then those one branded "Conad", all widespread on a large part of the municipal territory.

In referring to the details of the multiple precautionary measures, as a demonstration of this mafia, the investigation highlighted the interests of the 'ndrangheta and in particular of the territorial De Stefano-Tegano from the investigations converged into the sentence sent by the Court of Appeal of Reggio Calabria (No. 500/2008 RGA of 2.2.2009), against De Stefano Orazio Maria Carmelo, with whom explicit reference is made to the aforementioned Suraci as an intermediary of Orazio De Stefano and consequently the interests of mafia organization to which it belongs in the GDO business[31].

Sicily remains a territory in which the mafia evidence is even greater with reference to the GDO. For example, in October 2017, was arrested Giuseppe Ferdico, nicknamed the "king of detergents", of Palermo, to whom, already in March 2017, an active company in the GDO plus a series of assets valued at over 450 million euros were confiscated. Nevertheless, the judicial administrator appointed by the Court, the accountant Luigi Miserendino, has continued to manage the supermarkets and the shopping

---

31   In the aforementioned OOC, read together with that one no. 2/2012 (both issued in Proceeding No. 4614/2006/21 RGNR DDA), it emerges that this role, also through the conduct of fraudulent bankruptcy and aggravated fraud against the State, the dissipation of asset or the serious indebtedness of some companies, abandoned to themselves and then relaunching others, operating under a different brand and name, was carried out by Suraci through its participation and substantial control of numerous companies operating in the Gdo of Reggio market.

centre in Ferdico. For this reason both, together with three other people, were arrested by the financiers of the Palermo Tax Police with accusations of a fictitious heading of goods, personal and real aiding and extortion aggravated by the Mafia method.

The wiretapping clearly shows how Miserendino, who would have leased the mall to a nominee of the entrepreneur, knew that Ferdico continued to manage the seized property (from employee paychecks to the choice of suppliers). Miserendino had been appointed as judicial administrator by the former president of the prevention measures of the court, Silvana Saguto, who was later investigated for corruption in the context of an investigation into the mismanagement of confiscated assets. In this case, however, Saguto had imposed on the judicial administrator a series of obligations and checks on the activities of Ferdico that Miserendino has ignored.

The D.A., in fact, also contends the violation of the magistrate's measure. Ferdico, already tried and acquitted in 2014 by the accusation of competition in the mafia association, is considered by the investigators close to the mafia clan of San Lorenzo-Tommaso Natale and "socially dangerous".

What is represented here indicates not only the interest and the ability of the various mafias to penetrate and condition the GDO, but also their procedures, with managerial professionalism, with the aim of laundering illicit money, conditioning the policies of supply of goods and products, of the relative prices and to hide, in the complex articulated of companies that make up the Gdo in Italy, own societies or societies with own nominees, widening the territorial spectrum of own competence up to comprise substantially new territorial realities as some region of the North of the Country.

IV   In Italy, logistics, which includes transport, warehousing and transport support, is one of the most important sectors for the national economy, with about 1 million employees for 123,000 active businesses[32] (about 7% of the total employees employed in the business economy and 3% of all active companies).

A more detailed analysis of the sector shows a structure of the sector characterized by the prevalence of small and medium-sized companies (48% of road haulage and storage companies in Italy do not exceed 9

---

32   ISTAT – Business Report – Last data available year 2015. Source: https://www.
     istat.it/it/imprese

employees, while those with a number of employees equal to more than 250 represents only 0.02% of the total), also in the form of cooperatives, which often operate at the local level on the commission of large international groups. It is clear that an efficient transport sector supports economic growth, facilitating trade in goods and making businesses competitive, while consumers can buy products at lower prices[33]. Yet, the average cost of transport in the country is on average at a higher level than the economic realities present in other European countries. According to a study carried out by Nonisma – a company of economic studies, in fact, the mileage cost of road transport is on average higher in Italy (1.59 euros) than in countries such as Germany (1.35 euros), France (1, 32 euros) and Spain (1.21 euros).

In this context, it is appropriate to highlight the particular modus operandi of the mafias to infiltrate the national logistics. In fact, through direct control of minor transport companies, or through extortion and intimidation activities, the mafia associations effectively manage to govern the market and obtain huge profits. In the field of trucking, the mafia link between the clans and some companies is an expression of very intense patronage relationships, lived in terms of loyalty and respect towards the boss, until the identity of the mafia enterprise is identified.

The mafia conditioning in this sector is not at all recent. We find investigations, seizures and arrests by the Magistracy and the police from the early seventies of the twentieth century. As an example, we can mention the case of Cittanova's mafia boss, an important centre of Gioia Tauro's Plain, in Calabria, which, at the beginning of his entrepreneurial activity, ie around the early seventies, was responsible for the transport of citrus products. and building material. According to the Magistrature, he "with his mere presence, made any competitor" move away from his sphere of activity, demonstrating that this sector constituted not only an occasion for money laundering of illicit origin but also a mafia strategy planned to appropriate a Nerve sector for the affirmation and consolidation of the agro-mafias in Italy. Another example concerns the case of two northern hauliers killed in the Gioia Tauro's Plain in 1979[34]. The two drivers were employees of the company "Eva" of Verona, which had concluded mutually beneficial agreements with some groups of citrus fruit producers of the Gioia Tauro's Plain, in Calabria, endangering the power of the mafia entrepreneurs and local exporters related to the 'ndrangheta which monopolized the citrus

---

33   We can think about the development of e-commerce, mainly due to the improvement of logistic services, which allows the customer to obtain goods purchased online quickly and at reduced prices compared to in-store sales.

34   In "La Gazzetta del Sud", 5-6 january 1979.

cycle of the province of Reggio Calabria. These agreements, in fact, allowed the purchase of the agricultural product, in this case citrus fruit, up to 30-40% less than the average market price.

The relationship between trucking and mafias is even more evident with reference to some traditional mafia clans. According to the investigations of the judiciary, among these one, we mention the Pesce clan, which controls the main source of wealth of the city of Rosarno, Calabria Tyrrhenian, and the Magistracy defines "smart and clever criminals, monopolized the citrus trade, and with it the power over citizenship also influencing political activity"[35]. After terrorizing the possible competitors with bomb attacks and other intimidation actions, "the clan has monopolized the construction sector and the road haulage sector, directly exercising such activities or taking substantial shareholdings of profits from the owners of the various companies"[36].

In addition to the mafia control are the illicit phenomena related to the exploitation of workers and tax evasion. The investigative activities showed that organized crime intervenes in the field of road haulage, especially through the extortion of sums of money, the purchase of goods from suppliers imposed, the forced recruitment of personnel and the sale of business units. Another important aspect emerged following complex investigations that revealed original practices starting from the establishment of ever more extensive forms of cooperation between the various mafia organizations. It is important to mention the operations "Gea" and "La Paganese", described below, which have uncovered agreements, subtended to manage the sector in question, between Camorra clans and Sicilian Mafia.

In more detail, in November 2011, the State Police, together with the D.I.A. of Rome, Naples, Palermo and Trapani, as part of the operation conventionally called "La Paganese", has implemented a precautionary custody order, ordered by the GIP of the Court of Naples against 9 subjects, belonging to different mafia organizations operating in Campania and Sicily[37]. The activity, which originates from the "Sud Pontino" operation,

---

35   Carabinieri of Reggio Calabria, Carabinieri Legion of Catanzaro. Group of Reggio Calabria. Criminal Association in a mobster way of 260 person operating on the jonico side in the province of Reggio Calabria and other of the North and Central Italy, vol. IV, 1980, p. 1587.

36   Carabinieri of Reggio Calabria, Carabinieri Legion of Catanzaro. Group of Reggio Calabria. Criminal Association in a mobster way of 101 plus 19 person operating on the jonico side in the province of Reggio Calabria and other of the North and Central Italy, voll. 1-2, 1979, p. 29.

37   In particular, the ordinance of provisional detention concerned Gaetano Riina, who was already detained, accused of an external competition in the Mafia

has allowed the reconstruction of a whole decade of history of the economic and business relations between the Sicilian Mafia and the Camorra. The investigations confirmed the existence of a division of the business within the fruit and vegetable markets by the aforementioned mafia organizations, as well as the monopoly of the road transport sector by the Casalesi clan, allied with the Sicilian mafia. The investigative developments have made it possible to ascertain the significant advantages acquired by the criminal organizations in question, consistent, for the Casalesi, in the monopolistic management of an agency, "la Paganese", which controlled all the transport of fruit and vegetables related to the markets of Palermo, Trapani, Catania, Gela and Fondi. The Sicilians, on the other hand, enjoyed free access to their products in the markets of Campania and Lazio, with a predominance compared to other operators in the same sector. Following the transaction, in March 2014, after three years of hearings, the trial ended with 9 convictions. In July 2015, the D.I.A. of Rome, together with that ones of Naples, Salerno, Palermo, Caltanissetta, Catania and Bologna, as part of the operation conventionally called "Gea", has executed an order for preventive detention, issued by the GIP of the Court of Naples after the request of the local DDA, against 20 subjects, considered responsible for crimes of mafia association, illicit competition with threats or violence and extortion. At the end of the judicial police operation, 10 transport companies were subjected to seizure, these were attributable to the suspects, for a total value of approximately 100 million euros.

The operation is inspired by the aforementioned "Sud Pontino" survey, concluded by the D.I.A. in 2010 with over 60 arrests, the outcome of which was possible to discover the monopolistic management by the Casalesi and Mallardo clans, in collaboration with Cosa Nostra in Catania, of supplies of fruit and vegetables and the imposition of road transport services by and for the major markets of central and southern Italy. Such investigative activities have allowed, among other things, to outline the infiltration

---

association for having favored the Camorra association of Casalesi, and Nicola Schiavone, son of Sandokan, accused of illicit competition for having imposed the company 'La Paganese', controlled by his family, excluding all companies operating in the field of road transport to and from the fruit and vegetable markets of Sicily, Calabria, Campania and Lazio. Among the others arrested are also the brothers Antonio and Massimo Sfraga, Sicilian agricultural entrepreneurs and major Italian producers of melons, defined by the investigators as entrepreneurs linked to Cosa Nostra and in particular legitimized to exercise supremacy in their commercial sector on the basis of a privileged and personal relationship with the Riina family and with the innermost circle of entrepreneurs and men of honour that revolve around the famous fugitive Matteo Messina Denaro.

methods of the aforementioned criminal associations in the road transport system of agri-food products traded in the main fruit and vegetable markets of Campania, Sicily and Lazio. In essence, criminal societies imposed on the dealers the carriers to be used, attributable to companies directly expressing them, limiting, in this way, the system of free competition.

As for the Financial Police, further investigative activities are reported which confirmed the constant interest of the mafia organizations towards the sector in question. In 2011, for example, the P.E.F. of Milan, together with ROS dei Carabinieri, concluded the operation conventionally called "Redux-Caposaldo", which made it possible to ascertain the infiltration of the 'ndrangheta in the Lombard road transport system. The operation, which led to the arrest of 35 people, in various ways linked to the 'ndrangheta, as well as the seizure of assets for a total value of 2 million euros, has allowed to detect the particular interest of' ndrangheta in the sector of postal address. Specifically, it has been ascertained that TNT, an international giant in the transport sector and winning tenders for delivery and shipment of packages and parcels in the Lombardy region, subcontracted the postal service to cooperatives and local companies, equipped with their own means of transport. Through the direct control of these cooperatives and companies, therefore, the 'ndrangheta would have in fact obtained the monopoly in the management of the shipping service in the region.

In the months of April and June 2013, in two separate interventions, the Unit P.E.F./G.I.C.O. of Palermo seized as evidence two companies operating in the transport sector, for a total value of about 9 million euros, formally headed to nominee but, actually, attributable to an entity from Palermo, already convicted of mafia association and aggravated extortion by art. 7 of the D.L. 152/91 and arrested in 2011 as considered organic of the Brancaccio family;

In the period May 2014 – April 2015, the Unit P.E.F./G.I.C.O. of Reggio Calabria, as part of the transaction conventionally called "Total reset", has implemented twelve decrees, with which the Court of Reggio Calabria has ordered the seizure and confiscation of a large wealth, estimated at about 21 million euros, consisting of numerous movable and immovable assets, including three companies operating in the transport sector.

The patrimony was considered the result of the many criminal activities committed by the organs of the summit and relevant affiliates of the association of 'ndrangheta called "Pesce clan of Rosarno", hegemon in the "Gioia Tauro's Plain", with important and rooted operational ramifications on whole the national territory and abroad. Within the activity, the imposition of the personal prevention measure of special public security surveillance has been ordered with mandatory to stay in the municipality of residence and the payment of a cash deposit against 12 members, belonging to the above-mentioned clan. among which appears the person responsible for illicit investments in Lombardy and abroad.

In January 2017, in Licata (AG), Parma, the Financial Police (Palermo PEF / GICO Nucleus and PEF Nucleus of Agrigento), at the end of economic-patrimonial investigations ordered by the Court of Agrigento, seized assets for a total value over € 1.8 million, including several construction companies, road transport and stone crushing companies, with locations in Licata (AG) and in the province of Parma, resulting attributable to an entity from Agrigento already arrested in 2012 due to aggravated extortion and a fictitious heading of assets, which is part of the Mafia family of "Campobello di Licata" (AG).

In October 30, 2017, the Unit P.E.F./G.I.C.O. of Reggio Calabria, by the disposition of the Court of Reggio Calabria, has executed a seizure order against a company located in the same Calabrian municipality, manager of road transport activities, for a total value of more than three million of euros.

The company, the object of seizure and falsely headed to a nominee, turned out to be of a Reggio entrepreneur operating in the road transport sector, a leading exponent of a well-known clan of 'ndrangheta, active in the same province of Reggio. For the same reason the same company was already addressed, during 2015[38], a seizure and confiscation order, the latter revoked in October 2016.

The social danger of the entrepreneur and his prominent role in local organized crime have been established in the context of complex investigative operations, that ensued over time and aimed at striking the aforementioned clan of 'ndrangheta.

In particular, reference is made to the "Reggio Sud" operation, in which the Unit P.E.F./G.I.C.O. above-mentioned and the R.O.N.I. of the Provincial Command of the Carabinieri of Reggio, at the end of a complex investigative activity, in 2013, they performed 33 personal restrictive measures against subjects deemed responsible for criminal association, including the aforementioned entrepreneur and the preventive seizure of a complex of movable and immovable assets and economic activities worth approximately 77 million euros.

---

38   Measures issued during 2015 at the conclusion of the investigations carried out by the Unit P.E.F./G.I.C.O. of Reggio Calabria, within the operations conventionally called "Tax Escape 2" and "Penelope".

Actions to combat this phenomenon have historically been delegated to the judiciary and law enforcement. In this sense, an active and conscious commitment on the part of the political forces and the ruling class of the country in general is lacking. In fact, it is the judiciary and law enforcement that have succeeded in intervening, given the regulatory instruments at their disposal, in the Italian transport and logistics system, with particular reference to the transport of fruit and vegetables, opposing, in terms of repression, mafias and clans of all kinds, with operations that have unveiled the mafia network and consequently the interests and relationships.

The infiltration of the mafias in the national road transport chain also affects the price dynamics of Italian fruit and vegetables, contributing to their increase, often disproportionate, finally released on the national agricultural system and on Italian citizens and consumers.

The Anti-Mafia Investigation Department, with its report on the activities carried out and results achieved in the first half of 2016, recognizes that "the sectors most affected (by mafias, ndr) were those ones related to construction, transport and agribusiness. In many cases, the surveys have also highlighted the activism of a vast gray area – made up of entrepreneurs, professionals, politicians and public officials – that contributes to the success of the mafia strategies. As it was found in numerous occasions, these subjects have made available their professionalism or their companies, in order to facilitate the association, benefiting for certain "services" (protection, liquidity, guarantees in the awarding of contracts) that in the early stages of the "agreement" it represents a kind of mafia start-up.

This is an evident conditioning, starting from some important operations of the Magistracy and law enforcement that have arrested mobsters involved in the transport sector and confiscated their assets. For example, we can mention the operation of the D.I.A. of Palermo that led to two seizures (decrees No. 3 bis / 2016 RMP of 9 June 2016 and No. 213/16 of the RMP of 21 December 2015) and a substantial confiscation of persons operating in the construction sector, as well as a confiscation against an entrepreneur in the transport sector (Decree No. 8/13 RMP issued on 20 January 2016).

This is not a strategy peculiar to the Sicilian mafia alone but, on the contrary, rather widespread and for this reason very dangerous for the integrity and efficiency of the country's transport chain. In fact, the Anti-Mafia Investigation Department, in fact, warns about the growing and increasingly professional interest of the Calabrian 'ndrangheta in the transport sector. It does not appear, in fact, accidental, declares the D.I.A. still in his report on the activity carried out and results achieved in the first half of 2016 "the shift of the interests of the clan from individual businesses – for example the control of bars, restaurants or hotels, however prestigious – to supply chain of the large commercial distribution, crucial in the social and entrepreneurial dynamics of any territory. In fact, it could envisage a strategy that is substantially similar to that already adopted in drug trafficking, ie an emancipation from "downstream" management – because it is more evident and less profitable – to prefer, on the contrary, "upstream" management of the economic sector to infiltrate, intercepting the fundamental points of the supply chain, whether linked to the transport sector, industrial logistics, construction, agro-food, health, tourism, energy or online betting, just to name some, whose value is growing in parallel with the opening of the international market frontiers. To this end, the subjects included in the 'ndranghetist network which, for historical reasons, has been structured over the years in the most disparate countries, could represent the guardians, more and more professionalized, of the described global economic interests".

A similar reflection can be made for the Casalesi clan, historically interested in the procurement and waste sector. It is no coincidence that this sector is the main cause of dissolution of local authorities, the last of which, in order of time, is the Municipality of Trentola Ducenta, dissolved ex art. 143 T.U.E.L. with the Decree of 11 May 2016, which took into account the judicial evidence that had shown the conditioning work exerted by the Casalesi clan, Zagaria group. In addition to procurements, the criminal areas of greatest interest for the Casalesi are represented – as the D.I.A still states, "From laundering, usury, extortion, betting management and online gambling and drug trafficking. With regard to the latter crime, whereas in the past criminality of Caserta was limited to acting as a mere investor, without intervening directly in the distribution and management of the store, in recent years it would have shown a greater interest in the active participation in traffic, in synergy with the associations of the nearby Neapolitan province. Furthermore, the interests of Casalesi, in addition to construction, the inactive cycle and catering, would fall on the large food distribution, logistics and transport".

Among the various judicial operations that have been successful over the last few years, the "Caronte" inquiry by magistrates Antonino Fanara and Agata Santonocito in Catania is cited. In the city of Etna the magistrates managed to clear the dome of road transports, carrying out 23 arrests and seizing a mafia treasure worth about 50 million euros. The men of the Ros, already in the Iblis proceeding, had crossed some key figures of the Caronte operation, starting from Francesco Caruso, intercepted during a meeting with Alfio Aiello, brother of the Catania mob boss, arrested in the Iblis operation for Mafia association. Caruso and Scuto "entertained, with confidence, – the investigators write – relations with mobsters and politicians, including Cristaudo and Lombardo (both involved and convicted at first instance for the Iblis investigation)". The ex president of the Region replied by stressing his strangeness to any kind of involvement.

Key figure in this investigation is that one of Enzo Ercolano, son of the historic boss of Catania Pippo Ercolano, brother of Nitto Santapaola, who, to increase their business, "would use the intimidating force" of his surname, facilitating the strengthening – from the point of view of the investigators – of excellent alliances of organized crime also in Palermo with entrepreneurs "presumably connected" to the Agrigento and Palermo mafia.

Cosa Nostra would have succeeded through the creation of consortia to focus the control also to perceive the so-called ecobonus. The two affiliated entrepreneurs would not miss this opportunity to make money and would also contact administrators and politicians to speed up their practices. The control of meat sales would have taken place, instead, through agreements and the fictitious heading of some companies to a Calabrian entrepreneur. Moreover, the involvement of Vincenzo Aiello, the provincial referent of the clan, and of his brother Alfio, would also appear. Aiello's "boys" would have continued to operate even after the arrest of their boss "interweaving relations with other members of the organization and also engaging in extortion activities and control in the sale of meat in large retailers". According to the Ros's investigation, the companies belonging to Enzo Ercolano would have been involved in the transport of materials for the construction of the new local Agri-food Market, the largest wholesale commercial structure in the South. The contacts between Enzo Ercolano and a lawyer, president of the Board of the Maas, to participate in the private negotiation of the works for the construction of a logistic platform, also emerge from the Ros's investigations.

Unveiling the relationship between the Camorra and the Mafia with reference to the logistics of the Italian fruit and vegetable sector was an investigation done by the Naples DDA which led to the confiscation of assets worth over 1.8 million euros by the Anti-Mafia Investigation Department of Trapani, attributable to a 50-year-old entrepreneur from Marsala. Thanks to this investigation, Dia has identified a pact between the Camorra clan of the Casalesi and the brother of Totò Riina, Gaetano, to control the transport of fruit and vegetables from Rome to the whole South.

The main work activity of the Catania entrepreneur has always been that one of the transport. "Free from convictions for acts of the Mafia, its inclusion in the underworld and the adherence to the mafia logics of management of economic initiatives is linked to his role as administrator (as a" nominee "), within the transport company called" AFM Autofrigo Marsala Soc. Coop "in which the mobster exponent from Marssala Ignazio Miceli, already under special supervision of whose patrimony, post mortem, was ordered to confiscate from the Court of Trapani, always proposed by the Director of Dia", explain the investigators. The transport company has also been at the center of a judicial inquiry conducted by the Neapolitan Dda on mafia infiltration in the circuit of the large fruit and vegetable distribution of the Pontine countryside.

The investigators have discovered within the Fondi fruit and vegetable market, one of the main ones in Italy and in Europe, "the existence of a division of the business by the underworld organizations operating in the area and a monopolization of the road transport sector of the Casalesi clan". Those investigations have unveiled "the infiltration and conditioning of the clan" of the Casalesi-wing Schiavone "in the activities of the main fruit and vegetable markets, and also highlighted that the Casalesi clan, in order to win exclusive control in the strategic transport sector of fruit and vegetables products on the routes to and from Sicily, had made a real alliance with entrepreneurial delegates of Sicilian Cosa Nostra headed by Gaetano Riina, brother of the boss Totò Riina, located in the province of Trapani for years." Main beneficiary, on the Sicilian side of the province of Trapani, of the mafia business agreement between the Camorra players of the" Casalesi "and the mobsters from Trapani would have been the" A.F.M. Autofrigo Marsala ", managed by Miceli and Gagliano", the investigators say. Among the confiscated assets are numerous land and buildings, the entire capital and the business compendium of a trucking company based in Mazara del Vallo, vehicles and bank accounts, for a value of over 1.8 million euros.

In September 2018, however, reports and interests of the mafias in the Italian logistics system emerged again with reference in particular to the Fruit and Vegetable Market of Fondi. The DDA of Rome, in fact, together with the carabinieri of the provincial command of Latina, have executed among Fondi, Terracina and Mondragone six arrests and under accusation is ended, once again, d'Alterio family from Fondi, long considered by the magistrates and investigators referring to the Casalesi clan. The corporate assets and the shares of the transport company "La Suprema srl" were also seized. According to the Anti-mafia, the suspects are responsible, in various ways, for extortion, use of money of illegal origin, competition with threat or violence, fraudulent transfer of values, fictitious heading of goods and self-laundering, crimes committed with the aggravating circumstance of the mobster method. The investigation, called "Aleppo", began after some investigations carried out by the Carabinieri of Fondi and was finally continued by their colleagues in the Investigative Unit. For the Anti-mafia, the D'Alterio would have controlled the proceeds of the Mof, thanks also to the "deep connections with the Camorra clans from Caserta". In fact, it would have exercised "an intimidatory power of mafia type" with the aim of monopolizing transport from and to the Mof, also imposing its own "tax" on the movements made by other companies, taking control of the company "La Suprema", fictitiously registered to a nominee but managed in fact by the sons of Giuseppe D'Alterio, known as 'the Moroccan', bypassing the measures of patrimonial prevention and threatened an entrepreneur in the province of Viterbo, to recover his assets that this entrepreneur had purchased at a public auction after these assets had been removed from D'Alterio in implementation of a preventive measure. D'Alterio, after having been repeatedly investigated for drug trafficking, with drugs hidden between fruit and vegetables directed to Mof, and also for the marketing of infected meat with exponents of the Mafia family Rinzivillo of Gela, is considered by the investigators one of the main architects of the mafia business carried out around the Mof, above all by imposing firms and prices for fruit and vegetable transport. A sector in which, in addition to the Casalesi, would have dominated the Tripodo, sons of the mob boss don Mico, condemned at the end of the "Damascus" process and protagonists of the investigations that ten years ago took twice to ask for the dissolution of the municipal council of Fondi for mafia, even if needlessly, first the prefect of Latina and subsequently the then interior minister, Roberto Maroni. At Mof, after these investigations, the D'Alterio and the Casalesi families would settle down, also forcing business with Cosa Nostra and with the brother of Totò Riina (Gaetano). In the space of twenty years there have been numerous attacks, including injuries and fires, which have marked the mafia domination of the business linked to the fruit and vegetable market.

The recent "China Truck" operation carried out by the police, delegated by the District Anti-Mafia Prosecutor's Office in Florence, in various Italian cities and abroad, has allowed the arrest of 33 people accused of criminal association. The operation has routed a Chinese mafia organization that acted as well as in Italy, in various other European countries. Approximately 130 policemen of the Central Operations Service and of the mobile teams of Prato, Rome, Florence, Milan, Padua and Pisa, 18 patrols of the crime prevention department of Florence and Rome, the dog handlers Unit of Bologna and the Flight Department of Florence and

Rome were engaged. The French and Spanish police also collaborated. The investigation, which started in 2011 and conducted by the policemen of the Prato mobile team and the central operational service, involved a criminal association that asserted its hegemony in the control of the traffic of goods by road throughout Europe, hegemony in the field of logistics imposed by mafia methods and fuelled by revenue from criminal activities typical of the Chinese underworld. The criminal organization, composed by subjects originating in some Chinese regions such as Zhejiang and Fujian, operated not only in Italy but throughout Europe and stated its supremacy by subjecting companies of Italians operating in the same sector in Prato, Rome, Padua, Milan, Paris, Neuss (Germany) and Madrid, through intimidation and violence. 54 people were investigated, including 33 prisoners of protective measure in jail issued by the CPS Alessandro Moneti, on request by Florence DDA, for criminal association of mafia and other crimes, while another 21 people were investigated, in a state of freedom, and among these ten people always for criminal association and eleven for other crimes.

Another important operation named "Gold Transport Single-member" involved a limited liability company in Reggio Calabria seized from the Calabrian Financial Police, by order of the District Anti-Mafia Directorate. Overall seized assets amount to an estimated value of 3 million and 15 thousand euros. The owner of the company at the time it started the transaction, would have detected it in 2016 after the same company had been put under preventive seizure and then confiscated the previous year. In the Reggio Sud and in others called Tax Escape 2 and Penelope, which led to 33 detentions and the seizure of assets for 77 million euros, the two Ficara brothers were implicated, ex owners of the company: Giovanni, currently detained and considered one of the summits of the Ficara-Latela gang of the 'ndrangheta, and Domenico, owner of the "Gold Transport". After the sale to the new owner, the Court of Appeals of Reggio Calabria on request by Ficara lawyers revoked the confiscation. To give a new input to the Public Prosecutor allowing the seizure would be the statements of a third brother, who would have told the investigators that the "Gold Transport", even after the sale of 2016, was in the availability of his brother Domenico and in this way he had obtained exclusively to move the goods of an active company in the wholesale area in Reggio. In practice, in accordance with the links in both companies, mobsters had succeeded to obtain an exclusive contract and to transport with a particularly advantageous margin for the road transport company that was formally sold to a third person, but which actually continued to manage with considerable earnings.

The effects of this conditioning system of the road haulage mafias are discounted on the prices of agricultural products, with consequent growth of the same, and on consumers, forced to pay high prices for products that would cost less. This is a problem of great importance. "Fruit and vegetables are underpaid to farmers on values that do not even cover production costs, but prices multiply up to 300% from field to table, also due to the monopolistic control of the markets operated by underworld in certain territorial realities – Coldiretti claims – The most sensitive points for criminal infiltrations are the road transport services of fruit and vegetables to and from the markets; by the ancillary companies (indirect extortions such as the imposition of boxes for packaging); from the falsification of the origin traces of fruit and vegetables (such as the falsification of labelling: in this way, products from North Africa are passed off as EU); from the anomalous level of price growth due to brokerage carried out by the commission agents through mixed forms of production, storage and marketing, according to the National Anti-Mafia Directorate". "To achieve the goal – continues Coldiretti – the clans resort to all types of traditional crimes: usury and extortion racket, but also to theft of equipment and agricultural means, cattle rustling, illegal slaughtering or damage to crops by cutting entire plantations. Not only do they take advantage of large sectors of the agro-food sector and the profits deriving from it, destroying competition and the free legal market and stifling honest entrepreneurship – concludes Coldiretti – but they also seriously compromise the quality and safety of products".

3.
IMMIGRATION, AGRICULTURAL WORK, AND THE "NEW SOCIAL MATTER"

FIAMMETTA FANIZZA

I   Beyond the emerging humanitarian aspect, the measures concerning immigration that the Italian government has thus far launched in synergy with numerous local, institutional, and social players have unfortunately been ineffective and inadequate in fulfilling the following goals:

- Obtaining meaningful results in terms of receiving and including immigrants on a socio-territorial level;
- Dealing with conditions of marginalization and social deprivation both in communities and their living and working environments.

Generally unprepared to accept immigration as a phenomenon affected by historical and political conditions and events, the measures introduced in Italy have not managed to change from a methodological approach or in the implementation of intervention tools. The reluctance of Italian policies to adopt more adequate solutions regarding the regulation of migratory fluxes is also reflected in the weak response to the problems linked with unregulated labour.

Trapped in a mindset characteristic of the late nineteenth century, Italian immigration policies have been slow to identify a paradigm in which to elaborate national strategies. Even the European Union has erroneously adopted a Darwinist perspective and neocolonialistic strategy. Without an effective plan of action, the EU inexplicably continues to hope that the migratory contingents will stop, therefore putting an end to the legitimate requests for help from the European countries receiving the immigrants – with Italy at the top of the list – and the expectations of the immigrants' countries of origin. However, in dealing with both the immigrants' desire for a better future as well as the problem of human traffickers, the European Union's actions and previsions have been anachronistic and have ultimately failed. The immigrants' opportunities for a better life and a bright future have been crushed by the criminal work and opportunistic calculations of human traffickers.

Given the inexplicable abscondence of European institutions, the authors of this essay deem the measures introduced in Italy inadequate after an evaluation of the limited ability of Italian governments to implement social innovation, or in other words to recognize the effect of economic globalization and manage the processes of transformation caused by the dynamics of immigration.

Despite the fact that the situation can be objectively and statistically classified as structural, the considerable presence of immigrants in Italy has not yet been dealt with as a consolidated and, in certain ways, irreversible reality. Therefore, continuing to manage fluxes without paying attention to the new human geographies produced by transitions and reconfigurations of political and social structures, the approach of Italian public policies on immigration is still characterized by a transitory and short-term nature. Aside from its failure to improve society and integrate foreigners, this approach has shown itself to be inadequate when Europol investigations revealed that employing migrant workers allows criminal and mafia organizations to increase in power and influence and become a system capable of branching out and extending business and methods beyond the national territory, that is to establish roots through agreements founded upon the necessities required by the rules of the globalization of markets.

Regarding *caporalato* specifically, the fact that it is reinforced and consolidated by the segregation and enslavement of immigrants has brought about the brutalization of agricultural production through speculative and intensive use of the lands. Aside from the violation of human rights and freedom, this brutalization has led to the impoverishment of agronomic heritages and fauna. In addition to economic and environmental damage, this brutalization has contributed to the dismantling of the socio-anthropological value of rural culture, which characterizes the history of Italian demographic growth, assigning meaning to places as well as specific and complex identities to the communities and landscapes in which they live.

Since the end of the 1950s in the midst of hurried and irregular industrialization processes first and foremost from a geographical point of view, the concentration of immigrants confined to the countryside has contributed to the definitive dismantling of rural culture. In this regard, certain territories and rural areas have become permanently off-limits to most Italian citizens since, in addition to ghettos and camps, the constellations of shacks and residential structures in many isolated and entrenched areas (especially in southern Italy) are not merely a seasonal phenomenon. Therefore, above all because of the living conditions forced on the immigrants, life in the countryside is increasingly associated with situations of abandon, which in the collective imagination become almost a sort of social punishment in contrast with living in the community typical of urban contexts. Rural territories, in summary, are thus considered a sort of "no man's land" that are particularly vulnerable in their positions of absolute disparity because of the effects of the diffusion of the phenomenon of the globalization of the farmlands, namely because this phenomenon is connected to the presence of agromafias and their control of the farmlands. As a result, those who live or spend time there are forced to endure the stigma of having been abandoned, or worse, of being considered an individual who is forced to put up with the presence of organized crime. In this case, the individual must deal with and/or come to an agreement with the criminal organizations in the territory – above all in southern Italy – if he is in the agricultural business. At any rate, being "abandoned" and left to live in the countryside implies being condemned to being invisible and disconnected socially as well as deprived of one's identity. Thus abandonment, disconnection, and deprivation have become the key elements of a cultural dismantling that, from a historical point of view, explains very relevant social consequences. An example of this can be found in many regions in southern Italy where industrial expansion is still irregular due to an irrational and irresponsible underestimation of the agricultural sector.

In light of these scenarios, the possibility of combining immigration and economic development policies is one to be taken seriously. The thesis of this essay is essentially this: just as an investigation into the problems of the immigrants' living conditions cannot be ignored, a strategy to combat *caporalato* must study at length the reasons and mechanisms of the hybridization of ineffective economic processes connected to real objectives of change, development, and innovation. In this perspective, starting with the presupposition that the "ghetto system" allows for a productive model that in certain ways resembles the proto-industrial model denounced by social investigations in the mid-1800s, it is advantageous that the analysis of the immigrants' and locals' living conditions be combined with an examination of the productive successes, economic objectives, and territorial potential for economic growth and development. Moreover, given the gravity of the problems and difficulties caused by the considerable agromafia presence, this proposal must dutifully ponder if the "ghetto system" is not perhaps the most evident symptom of a "new social matter" that concerns the need to promote a shared and involved management of public resources. In the event of an affirmative response, the fight against *caporalato* must concentrate on the ability of local systems to better allocate skills and use them to increase social capital.

The reference to a "new social matter" grasps the urgency expressed not only by sociological studies but also by statistical data to once again guarantee the wellbeing of individuals, populations, and territories. Essentially it is a "matter" of:

- Researching solutions to economic instability and precarious employment;
- Avoiding all forms of political and social marginalization and exclusion;
- Electing the principle of sustainability to orient the method for managing public resources and accumulate collective heritages.

Strictly connected with both the problem institutions have of defending the territory and the problem of protecting extremely vulnerable social-territorial capital, this "new social matter", even more than an economic impact, has value for the social identity as a red flag, so to speak, indicating some problematic knots, including the following:

- The difficult correlation between multifunctional local development and environmental regeneration processes;
- The identification of methods of autopoiesis and self-sustainment capable of contributing to the fine-tuning/finalization of suitable strategies to consider the territory as a true social heritage;
- The introduction of multicultural welfare systems.

To address the specific problems that emerge from the presence of immigrants, it is necessary to expand the vision and surpass the central and local Italian governments' mindset, which is focused on aid-based, local, and short-term solutions. The "new social matter" works toward the objective of direct responsibility regarding the management of differences and disparity. Above all, starting with the recognition of the problems linked to the different ethnicities and a particularly careful examination of the impact they have on the social and living organization of the local and native communities, it should deal with the following inequalities:

- Economic;
- Environmental;
- Social;
- Cultural.

With the intention of realizing equal opportunity for native citizens and immigrants, the "new social matter" would introduce a series of approaches and measures to create generative welfare, social innovation, and economic development. Above all, through the critical analysis of the reasons behind the fact that the ghetto system is indirectly assigned a crucial role in the symbolic management of conflicts produced by the presence of immigrants, the reflection on the logic that regulates the segregation system would provide the incipient to restore dignity to agricultural work and re-establish rights, reassigning esteem and the proper economic worth to the entire agricultural sector.

In order to evaluate the possibility of intervening in such a way as to allow a political strategy to bring about the wellbeing of individuals and territories through the reorganization of (material and relational) resources and skills, the need for an awareness of a "new social matter" emerges, particularly as one examines all the measures of welfare adopted by the Italian ministry of domestic affairs and the regional administrations concerning immigrants and integration/inclusion.

As a matter of principle, in an effort to integrate and include immigrants it is possible to distinguish two fundamental approaches adopted by different Italian governments over the course of the last twenty years. The first approach consists of "no action", or rather the uncontrolled and undisturbed proliferation of makeshift camps. Examples of this can be seen in the camps located in the Gioia Tauro Plain in the region of Calabria, especially in the town of San Ferdinando. Today almost two thousand people live in an abandoned paper mill[1], where rooms made of cardboard and bamboo measure 3 square meters. Another emblematic example can be found in the province of Foggia (also called Capitanata) in the region of Apulia. There the large number of settlements transforms the ghetto system into a true criminal hub. The presence of the ghettos is so widespread that, thanks to data and censuses by trade union association FLAI-CGIL with geolocalization devices, it is possible to draw a map of those with the highest concentration. These include:

The "Large Ghetto in Rignano", only 13 kilometres from Foggia;
The "Macciarotonda ghetto" in the countryside in San Severo;
The "Bulgaria ghetto" in Stornara;

---

1   The establishment belongs to *Modul System Sud*, a company from Emilia-Romagna that ceased operations a few years ago and abandoned the barn.

- The "Ghana ghetto" and "Borgo Tressanti ghetto", located in the city of Cerignola;
- The "Siros ghetto" in the town of Ortanova.

Fig. 1: Georeferencing map of Foggia. Source: FLAI CGIL

One must add to these the constellation of rural farmsteads in the towns of Mafredonia, Zapponeta, and San Marco in Lamis and the camps set up in the rural hamlets of Segezia and Incoronata in the city of Foggia or along the old military airport in Borgo Mezzanone on the outskirts of Manfredonia.

The second type of approach is represented by so-called "unfulfilled action" and consists in the realization of tent cities on the extreme outskirts of rural centres. For example, in San Ferdinando, Calabria, in the autumn of 2016 a tent city was set up to house 1,500-1,700 foreign labourers. As was unfortunately foreseeable, hundreds of makeshift shacks sprang up around the tent city. In fact the tent city has become the main body of a new ghetto above all due to the complete lack of services like portable chemical toilets.

In Apulia, an example of "unfulfilled action" is seen in the *alberghi diffusi*, another type of housing accommodation for immigrants, which the Apulia Department of Social Policies fought for and financed in 2008-2010.

The *alberghi diffusi* represent an experimental model of accommodation for immigrant workers in structures equipped to offer basic services (basic healthcare, literacy teaching, legal advice, basic training in agricultural work, socialization among guests). They were designed exclusively for immigrants in possession of a work permit or other legal documents, and, in order to pay for the management of the structures, the immigrants were asked to pay a nominal price usually for food vouchers or use of the rooms. This payment, aside from favoring participation in the management of the structures, was a way to give the immigrants responsibilities with the goal of creating new employment opportunities within the *alberghi diffusi*.

Despite excellent intentions, the failure of these structures was caused by the fact that in order to accommodate thousands of immigrants a different mindset and approach was necessary even though the efforts and use of *best practices* were truly commendable. Indeed, despite the firm commitment, only three structures were built:

- In Torre Giuducci (Foggia) with a capacity to house 42;
- In Borgo Tressanti (Cerignola), capacity of 50;
- In Casa Sankara (San Severo), capacity of 41.

In addition to the failed *alberghi diffusi*, in Apulia the unfulfilled action regards the construction of tent cities, which re-emerges cyclically. To solve the problem of the violation of human rights and combat *caporalato*, two regional legislations, *Delibera 574 "Capo free – Ghetto Off"*[2] dated 2 April 2014 and the more recent *Piano Triennale per le Politiche Migratorie 2016-2018*[3] (The Three Year Plan of Policies on Immigration in the Region of Apulia[4]), both consistently turn to tent cities as the remedy still put into practice today.

Delibera 574 "Capo free – Ghetto Off" was created as a transitory measure to house immigrants from the "Large Ghetto in Rignano"[5] after

---

2 To read the legislation, see *Regione Puglia Deliberazione della Giunta Regionale N. 574 DEL 02-04-2014, Codice Cifra: PGI/DEL/2014/00006, Struttura Proponente: Servizio Politiche giovanili e cittadinanza sociale – Politiche per lo sviluppo economico, lavoro e..., Allegati: 574_2014_1.pdf (dim.: 210.66 kb – agg.: 07-04-2014), "Piano di azione sperimentale per un'accoglienza dignitosa e il lavoro regolare dei migranti in agricoltura. Documento d'indirizzo".*

3 The official bulletin of the Region of Apulia no. 23 dated 12 February 2018.

4 Hereafter referred to as the *Piano Triennale*.

5 Illegally managed for over fifteen years on land owned by the Region of Apulia, it is the largest tent city in the province of Foggia. This immense camp of shacks situated around a few dilapidated houses is occupied by African immigrants. It is

its closure. Since during the summer season this ghetto houses 1,500-2,000 people and throughout the year 350-500 people, the regional government had decided to construct three tent cities to be managed by the Red Cross. These structures have never been built both because of the resistance offered by those who even today continue to control the ghetto (and who at one point manifested their opposition by setting fire to the shacks, a frequent occurrence in the ghettos that is used as a method of intimidation to demonstrate the strength of the criminal organizations) and due to the slowness of local bureaucracy.

The failed logic of *Delibera 574 "Capo free – Ghetto Off"* has been replicated in the *Piano Triennale* in that it has the same intention (to dismantle the ghettos and restore dignity to the immigrants) and strategy to manage the tent cities (even though this time the idea was to involve various public participants – like educational institutions and the health department – as well as private organizations). Despite the involvement of many stakeholders, including the Universities of Foggia, Bari, and Lecce, the health department, and many non-profit organizations, even the *Piano Triennale* considered tent cities an adequate solution and utilized them as a resource above all in the dismantling of the various ghettos throughout Foggia and to provide transitory housing to those who had previously lived there. Therefore, although it is impossible to judge the efforts because the dismantling of the ghettos and the construction of the tent cities never began, doubt remains as to how effective and practical the project would have been. Therefore, the project is "unfulfilled" because it would have resolved, if anything, an emergency but does not represent the key to a new policy for accommodation and integration.

Given that the ghettos continue to exist and even now *caporalato* does not seem to suffer from the measures put in place by various laws, it is possible to conclude that neither approach is successful at preventing the ghettoization of immigrants. Moreover, the mindset of these approaches more or less mindfully and intentionally marginalizes foreign citizen and restricts agricultural production to a presumed and pretentious position of economic and cultural inferiority. As a result, since changing prejudices and discourse is certainly a difficult and gruelling task, the solution must be found in the availability of welfare approaches to operate and harmonize needs, dreams, and images of the future regarding people, territories, economic players, and political subjects.

---

located only thirteen kilometres from the city of Foggia and only ten kilometres from the city of San Severo.

Since the highest concentration of *caporalato* is found in the southern regions of Italy (Sicily, Calabria, Apulia, and Campania), the strategies to counter agromafias and the tools to integrate and include immigrants must first deal with the problem of reinstating legality. Otherwise, like the situation that occurred in Rosarno (Calabria) in 2012, the will to change will be destined to fail[6].

---

6   Beton Medma, a former cement plant located a mere six kilometres from the urban centre, was confiscated from 'Ndrangheta clans with the intention of converting it into small housing units for the 150 foreign citizens employed in the orange harvest. While it was still being constructed, the magistracy opened up an investigation under the suspicion that 'Ndrangheta had infiltrated and was controlling the construction company.

4.
ANTI-MAFIA ACTIVITY OF THE FINANCIAL POLICE IN 2017

Marco Omizzolo

I The activity of prevention and contrast against the phenomenon of "Gang masters", carried out by the Financial Police, has allowed to unveil and suppress numerous illicit conduct aimed at the exploitation of the weakest sections of the population and the deprivation of the fundamental rights of the individual.

In this context it is useful to retrace the main activities of the Corps departments to better outline the methods of carrying out illegal behaviour in terms of exploitation of the work and in particular understand the dangerous attitude of the dishonest or mobster entrepreneur, who in using intermediaries (caporals), takes advantage of the situation of socio-economic discomfort of defenceless workers. This is a reflection consistent with what has been analysed above because it highlights the modalities of action of the agro-mobster system and, on the other hand, the enforcement actions put in motion, in this case, by the Financial Police.

In this sense, the operation called "Paola", concluded in February 2017, by the Compagnia di Trani (in co-delegation with personnel of the Andria PS) and aimed at countering the complex phenomenon of "Gang masters", which implemented a precautionary order of custody ordered by the Court of Trani against 6 suspects accused, for various reasons, of fraud against the State and illegal intermediation and exploitation of labor. At the same time, the department has seized a sum equal to about 56,000 euros. The activity originates from the tragic event concerning the death of Paola Celemente, an Italian agricultural labourer, which took place on 13 July 2015 in a vineyard located in the agro area of Andria (BT). The subsequent investigations, also of a technical nature, together with the exhortation of people informed on the facts and the acquisition of documentation also from public offices, allowed to verify a widespread and well-established activity carried out by the investigated subjects.

Following the investigative activities carried out over the years[1] it has been possible to ascertain the increasing interest of criminal organizations in the management of labor exploitation. Earnings that are also fed in relation to the connected illegal activities of frauds against the State and social security institutions in order to obtain contributions that are not due. The involvement of the "mafias" does not concern only the stage of intermediation of work. The criminal organizations, in fact, involved in the activities of recruiting abroad of people to start working in the fields, in the delicate stages of transport and crossing the frontiers, to deal with their distribution in the territory according to the needs of employment and of actual exploitation, under conditions of complete deprivation of the most basic rights.

In this case, the phenomenon of "Gang masters" assumes even more serious connotations as the workers are subjected to particularly conditioning and violent and oppressive treatments by subjects that act with the typical mafia methods. A state of physical and moral subjection that effectively prevents any possibility of redemption for those subjects who, fleeing their country in the hope of a better future, find themselves in situations of serious exploitation and unacceptable living conditions[2].

Below are reported data referring to reports to the judicial authorities carried out in the course of 2017 by the Financial Police for the crime of "Illicit brokering and exploitation of labor" (Article 603 bis C.P.). It is appropriate to highlight the magnitude of the illicit cases indicative of irregular work situations, in which mainly migrant subjects are involved. This applies, in

---

1   We can consider the operation concluded in July 2016 by the District of Montegiordano, which made it possible to ascertain how certain agricultural entrepreneurs of Sibaritide turned to a "caporal" of Pakistani nationality, a result linked to two subjects belonging to the local clan, that "recruited" labourers to be exploited in agricultural activities, forcing them to work in total disregard of the most basic rules on safety in the workplace, organized the activity and paid them on the difference between what is perceived by the companies and how much actually paid to the workers.

2   *"... the conditions in which they are forced to survive, enduring the removal of personal documents, and the ghettoisation in makeshift structures subtracted, in fact, to the control of the police forces to which, often, access is forbidden, and governed, therefore, by the "caporals" backed by the mafia associations who exert a penetrating control over the guests aware of the blackmail power exercised by them, managing them the only form of livelihood of immigrants. Within the ghettos, the practice of prostitution and the trafficking of drugs are usually practiced.* " Parliamentary committee of inquiry about the phenomenon of mafias and other criminal associations, including foreign ones – Final report February 2018.

particular, to complaints made for violation of art. 12 paragraph 5 and of the art. 22 paragraph 12 of Legislative Decree. 25 July 1998 (Consolidated text of the provisions concerning immigration regulations and rules on the status of foreigners), which penalize the facilitation of the illegally of the foreigner and the employment by the employer of foreigners without a residence permit)[3]. The investigative findings underscore the close connection between the aforementioned illegal cases, making evident the vulnerability of the migrant in the condition of absence of residence permit to be exposed to the working exploitation by the criminal organizations.

VIOLATION	N. SUBJECT COMPLAINED
Art. 603 bis C.P. (illecit brokering and labour exploitation)	88
D.Lvo 25 july 1998, n. 286 art. 12, paragraph 5 (facilitating the conditions of illegality of the foreigner)	205
D.Lvo 25 july 1998, n. 286 art. 22 paragraph 12 and 12 bis (employment by the employer of foreigners without a residence permit)	89
Total	382

Table 1 – Subjects reported for crimes regarding "Gang-masters" and illegal immigration. Source: Statistical System of the Financial Police, year 2017.

The table shows that the main share of complaints to the judicial authority concerns individuals considered responsible for the crime of facilitating illegal immigration, while for the other two criminal offences, the percentage of people involved stands at 23% of the total reported. This of course is explained by the fact that the activity of aiding the illegal entry of migrants on the national territory has a multiplicity of purposes in addition to that of labor exploitation.[4]

The analysis of data relating to previous police data shows that most of the subjects involved in the aforementioned illegal cases of Gang-masters

---

3   In the analysis the subjects reported were considered. In the case, therefore, of more violations borne by the same subject, the data referring to the violation of Gang-masters (Article 603 bis C.P.) was considered, in order to avoid redundancies, in the accounting of the data.

4   Consider, for example, sexual exploitation.

and violation of immigration rules are reporting a wide range of further offences (extortion, trafficking of drugs, fraud, etc.). This demonstrates the criminal attitude of those involved in illicit brokering and labor exploitation. In particular it results that 20.42% of the subjects involved presents criminal record related to particularly serious criminal cases[5], that the anti-mafia legislation[6] indicates as a prerequisite for the application of personal and financial prevention measures.

Analysing the territorial distribution of the subjects involved in the "presupposed" crimes according to the domiciled residence, it is evident, once again, a widespread presence in almost all the regions, with the prevalence for Campania, followed by Lombardy and Lazio. A more detailed analysis of the data referred only to the criminal offence of "Illicit brokering and exploitation of labor, the c.d. "Gang-masters" (Article 603 bis C.P.), allows to highlight some particular aspects.

In the first place, the "Gang-masters" is no longer confined to the southern regions, traditionally interested in a strong rooting of criminal organizations, but involves with more or less intensity the entire national territory.

Another interesting aspect concerns the nationality of the subjects involved in the phenomenon. Data on the reports made by the Financial Police in the specific sector in the year 2017 show the clear prevalence of Italian subjects with 79% of the total number of complaints sent to the Judicial Authority, followed by individuals of Moroccan nationality with 15%. The data referring to subjects of other nationalities are modest, not exceeding 1% of the total number of subjects reported.

The investigative results testify the involvement of migrant workers in the phenomenon of Gang-masters, as in the case of February 2017 in which the Delegation of Montegiordano (CS) identified, as part of a control activity of vehicles in transit on the 106 jonica state road, two vehicles with twelve people on board, including seven Pakistani and one Senegalese people without a valid residence permit and a valid identification document. From the information acquired, it emerged their role as agricultural labourers, hired "payed under the table" by an entrepreneur and recruited by a "caporal" who brought them to the workplace. The latter, in addition to the work of labourers controlling, he provided to reduce the daily pay of 5 euros.

---

5   These are the crime sindicated in the art. 51 paragraph 3 bis of the Code of Criminal Procedure.
6   We refer to the D.lgs. September 6, 2011 n. 159 – *Code of anti-mafia laws and Preventive measures, as well as new provisions on anti-mafia documentation, pursuant to articles 1 and 2 of the law 13 August 2010, n. 136.*

The overall investigations carried out, which include the involvement of 3 agricultural companies and the identification of 8 workers "payed under the table", ended with the complaint to the competent judicial authority of 10 migrants for the facilitation and exploitation of the foreigner and violations in the matter of immigration. In July 2017, in Avola (SR), the Group of Siracusa concluded an articulated survey, coordinated by the local Public Prosecutor, against a farm responsible for the unlawful exploitation of non-EU workers. In particular, the agricultural company put in place illegal conduct of exploitation of workers in violation of regulations on work and rest, safety and hygiene of workplaces. The company, for the recruitment of workers, also used a "caporal" who, after picked them up on a van, took them to the fields. At the end of the activity the owners of the company and the "caporal" were reported to the judicial authorities for the crime of Gang-masters (article 603 bis c.p.). At the same time, the Court of Catania ordered the judicial control of the company and the consequent appointment of a judicial administrator.

The investigative activities confirm the central role of dishonest agricultural entrepreneurs in feeding the system of labor exploitation in order to benefit from cheap labor and thus obtain higher profit margins. The progressive worsening of the socio-economic conditions of the country, especially in the southern regions and the availability of an ever-increasing foreign labor force, without any protection, are the driving factors of the illegal labor market in agriculture.

In this context, criminal and mafia organizations acquire a paramount role, which, in managing the entire supply chain, satisfy the illegal labor demand, imposing inhuman conditions of life to exploited workers. The main victims of exploitation are the weakest sections of the workers, those who have an extreme need to obtain a salary, even a minimum and can not fully exercise their rights protected by the legislation in force. Among these, non-EU citizens, in conditions of clandestinity, represent the widest and most vulnerable category.

Ultimately, the phenomenon of exploitation is mainly attributable to subjects of Italian nationality, while the cases in which the protagonists of illegal intermediaries are foreign citizens still seem to be limited. We can therefore conclude that while on the one hand it is possible to recreate greater effectiveness and intensity of actions to combat the phenomenon in question, on the other hand there is a steady increase in situations of labor exploitation "in the fields", which is no longer confined to southern regions but now affects the entire national territory.

5.
INTEGRATION DEMAND AND NEW INCLUSION OFFERS

Fiammetta Fanizza

I   As the I.L.O. (International Labour Organization) announced in 2010, the housing problem is one of the most problematic aspects of immigration[1]. Furthermore, the I.L.O. has expressed concerns various times regarding the violation perpetrated in housing establishments and ghettos, calling attention to the absence of the bare minimum requirements in living conditions (water, electricity, and heating). The alarm raised by the I.L.O. is motivated by the fact that in many of these establishments segregation is a rule of life. Better said, living in these places means confinement in that the immigrants are deprived of liberties and are kept in a state of complete destitution. Even more, the immigrants run serious risks from a sanitary point of view, without considering that the absence of hygiene together with the absolute lack of medical care could represent a problem for the possible diffusion of disease or even epidemics that could threaten local as well as immigrant populations. While advising the Italian government to combat illegal immigration and at the same time protect the fundamental rights of irregular immigrant labourers, the I.L.O. expressly mentions the conditions of the immigrants exploited in Apulia and above all the grave situation in the province of Foggia.

The same warning was given by Doctors Without Borders[2]. According to the investigations and surveys conducted by this organization, the ghettos are the tip of the criminal iceberg. Doctors Without Borders maintains that the situations of territorial confinement are in fact the ideal conditions for exploitation. Therefore, reaching the same conclusions as the I.L.O.,

---

1   The I.L.O. (International Labour Organization) C143 – Migrant Workers (Supplementary Provisions) Convention, 1975 (No. 143), *Adoption: Geneva, 60th ILC session (24 Jun 1975)*.
2   On informal establishments, see the investigation by Doctors Without Borders published in 2016, http://www.asylumineurope.org/sites/default/files/resources/fuoricampomsf.pdf.

Doctors Without Borders shares the concern for the lack of research on ways of intervening and combatting agromafias.

Both of these organizations have been committed to collecting the data necessary to put an end to the exploitation of immigrant labourers and support the thesis that in order to deal with the issue of immigration, the following concepts must be acknowledged:

1. The immigrants' way of life determines the *caporali*'s ability to control the territory;
2. The analysis of the immigrant labourers' lodgings allows the morphology of the phenomenon of the globalization of the farmlands to be traced.

Both of these organizations strongly exhort the government to consider the theme of the agromafias and the conditionings that the territories are forced to undergo as central in the defining of migratory policies.

Although it is a reality that illustrates worrisome scenarios without escape, admitting the connection between criminality and immigration is a necessary step to begin the battle, which, according to social observers in the immigration and irregular employment sectors, requires greater visibility on the part of politicians and public opinion.[3] Denouncing this connection is strategic both to begin dismantling the mechanism of control of the spatial segregation systems and offer a new, different dialectic space within which to insert welfare projects that benefit immigrants and locals alike. Indeed, rather than continue to insist on a national security approach, it would be advantageous to look for new ways of understanding, interpreting, and combating the phenomenon of the agromafias, the problem of the exploitation of labour, and the effects of delayed economic development that exist despite the fact that for more than twenty years the European Union has invested millions of euros to finance and support the growth of production sectors in many Italian territories.

In addition to putting into practice the results of research and investigations conducted over the years, creating new social agreements – new because of their objectives, methods, and resources to invest – holds the potential to definitely change politics. It represents a choice to govern the complexity of the subject of immigration and at the same time provide an innovative vision on the topic of multicultural society.

---

3   Leogrande A. (2008), *Uomini e caporali. Viaggio tra i nuovi schiavi nelle campagne del Sud,* Mondadori.

Leaving aside personal judgement and moral opinions, our proposal is that of concentrating attention on the practical effects and the numerous implications produced by the presence of immigrants. The proposal naturally moves to implement intense and insistent activity to sanction all types of segregation, exploitation, and enslavement of immigrants. Condemning criminal activities would have an extremely important impact especially if the immediate advantages of dismantling the agromafias were demonstrated. With preliminary attention and priority on the economic and social advantages of putting an end to the exploitation of immigrants, the objectives of growth and development would find new resources both in funds no longer used by criminal organizations and new investments to guarantee greater employment and better profits.

The qualifying element of this proposal resides in the determination to fight agromafias and the urgency to experience innovative welfare approaches that are sufficiently able to unite needs and demands from various categories of subjects and interest bearers.

Among the original welfare formulas that help immigrants and locals, the model that the Region of Apulia is trying to realize following the emission of the *Piano Triennale* is of note. The regional legislature of Apulia has launched a series of innovative projects to activate various socialization practices with which to configure a new multicultural welfare model. Although it is an experiment that is in progress and thus it remains to be seen whether or not it will be successful, the philosophy behind the project is significant. Welfare in Apulia has become the guiding principle that allows both immigrants and locals to live better, or rather to live in contexts in which the problem of inclusion is dealt with through a synthesis of needs of the population, territories, and finally public and private institutions (the tertiary sector, religious organizations, schools, and universities).

The methodological approach of the *Piano Triennale* is founded on the will to surpass the concept of integration as a "cold" process. On the contrary, the identification of recipients/beneficiaries clearly shows the vision which keeps in mind that immigration is not a circumstantial event or an occurrence to sift through and deal with exclusively in the wake of quantitative considerations. The fluxes of immigrants are in fact an expression of human mobility determined by circumstances that can be related to violations of rights, difficult survival, or plans for individual betterment. Therefore, immigration requires the awareness that becomes practical in proceeding in the verification of the immigrants' right to reside in the regional/national territory.

By and large, the *Piano Triennale* drafted by the Region of Apulia concentrates on a concept of inclusion as a collective practice to develop in the environment of a continuous evolution of relationships between subjects: locals and immigrants, institutions and private parties. It is a practice for community that is profoundly oriented towards improving the living conditions of immigrants – on an individual level as well as ethnic community level – in addition to those of the citizens of Apulia on an individual and community level. Therefore, having declared the intention of going beyond the concept of integration which depends on the immigrants' acceptance of conditions predetermined by the hosting public administrations[4], this *Piano Triennale* aims to transform immigration into an opportunity to – finally – fix welfare, namely to move from a static concept of "social status" to a dynamic concept of "quality of life and social relationships". Thus, rejecting the idea of managing migratory contingents as an emergency, the verification of immigrants' rights to remain in the national territory represents the launching of a finalized path to producing benefits and advantages for the entire community.

Since it foresees along with projects for social integration for immigrants, asylum-seekers, refugees, victims of trafficking, violence, and slavery, active measures in politics for health and dignified living, the creation of new professional opportunities, and the increase of employment of vulnerable categories and particularly disadvantaged populations, the *Piano Triennale* proposes to surpass the classifications that refer to norms of welfare models[5]. In particular, it counts on a shared multicultural vision of society that corresponds to guidelines and choices aimed at the generation of new social and financial capital. Therefore, in the planning and division of resources agreed upon by the social parties involved including recipients and bearers of interests, the *Piano Triennale* counts on the advantages generated by the presence of foreigners and calculates these advantages in terms of reinforcing capacity building and broadening social dialogue[6]. As a result, it arrives at a different and more opportune distribution of

---

4   Kapezov J. and Carbone D. (2018), *Che cos'è il welfare*, Carocci. Roma, p. 109.
5   In short, it is possible to cite the following models:
     •   The French assimilation model, in which the immigrant is required full adhesion to values and ideals;
     •   The British pluralist model, in which cultural differences are admitted and mediation proceeds in order to guarantee homogenous access to democracy;
     •   The German "precarious" model, in which the foreigner remains a guest to whom *ad hoc* protection is provided on the basis of their diversity.
6   "Allegati – Studi" (Annexes and Studies) of the *Piano* conducted by IPRES, Institute for Economic and Social Research in Apulia.

material, immaterial, and human resources in order to resemble a "White Paper" for local welfare.

Interpreting coexistence through a dynamic project for the construction of new multicultural identity, Apulia's *Piano Triennale* rejects classic redistributive logic of "benefits for private collection" and vice versa interprets welfare as the generation of civil and even cultural growth processes. It naturally adopts a guiding philosophy that does not forget the real and concrete problems in the field. In fact, with the conviction that one of the most important problems that welfare must face is the inherent risk of occupational uncertainty and precarious employment, the *Piano Triennale* begins by deconstructing employment histories[7] in order to create social insurance plans that would improve the lives of locals and immigrants that live in Apulia. Building a map of skills present in the regional territory is not only a method to combat social vulnerability and orient investments in sectors where there is a greater demand for work. Adopting the "skills balance sheet" tool in order to know which immaterial resources are immediately available is above all a way to realize social empowerment. Within a framework where immigrants are not easily allowed to feel like real members of the population, social empowerment means that the knowledge of the social capital becomes a strategic factor to favour coexistence without conflict. In short, it is a way to react to and slow down those who insist they will not accept the immigrants' presence because they "steal work from Italians".

In order to offer equal opportunity employment in the fruition of rights within human and social contexts, it is important to consider the active work policies as social empowerment tools[8] just as it is important to establish cooperation between the categories of public and private interest bearers and activate community dynamics aimed at creating opportunities for the growth and development of human and social capital. Precisely through greater socialization, the *Piano Triennale* also attempts to connect public policies with the new demands for inclusion and naturally the typically social and aid-related materials such as the following:

- Public order and safety;
- Opposition to criminal activity linked to human trafficking, drug trafficking, and the exploitation of the prostitution of others;

7   Kazepov J. and Carbone D. (2017), *Che cos'è il welfare*, Carocci, Roma, p. 102.
8   Dryzek, J. (2010), *Foundations and Frontiers of Deliberative Governance*, Oxford University Press, NY.

- Defrauding the European Union;
- Evasion of legal employment regulations and tax obligations;
- Development of economic-productive districts.

Therefore, this *Piano Triennale* invests in socialization by leveraging the research on a popular *idem sentire* in the sense that people are engaged and effectively represented, or rather truly able to propose solutions to the problems of vulnerability and marginalization present in urban and rural contexts alike. For this reason, overcoming the tradition of agreeing upon opposing interests, it recommends confronting and discussing at length the method to achieve synthesis between individual and collective rights and to group together the needs of the community and social systems in order to generate greater social capital.

II   As in the region of Apulia, the combination of determining factors like geographic position, proximity to principle destination markets, and the existence of numerous infrastructures allows criminal organizations to weave international relations that are extraordinarily useful for their growth and expansion.

According to Europol sources, the maintenance of international relations in Apulia are safeguarded by the small and medium-sized businesses, or rather by a network of small and medium-sized agricultural businesses that daily fight or are involved in the criminal agromafia system. Nonetheless, the circularity and pervasiveness of the agromafia model requires these small and medium-sized businesses to utilize a business model focused on so-called "open" logic. In detail, these businesses are invited to enter and become part of a reticular system to control the territory. In this reticular system, every individual business becomes a "service junction". The grouping together of multiple junctions allows the agromafias to create a series of criminal hubs, each of which has a specialized role regarding the management of criminal activities that use the countryside and agricultural businesses as either an "ideal logistic location", a way to "finance" themselves, or a way to launder money. The extension and extremely wide spectrum of action of the Apulia network of service junctions, or so-called criminal hubs, is distinguished by its excellent dynamism and ability to communicate on an international level.

What is surprising about the Europol reports is that the agromafias use the Apulia countryside even in order to experiment with new methods and undertake new business. This possibility to experiment is made possible by the conditions of total liberty and impunity present in the countryside and also due to the widespread culture of illegality linked to the vast and numerous crimes of corruption and violation of human rights that do not allow the police force to intervene with the necessary promptness and incisiveness. What is worse is that in Apulia the misappropriation of public resources feeds the culture of illegality by slowing entrepreneurial growth with noteworthy repercussions on the political and social context. The result is a resigned or sceptical attitude, which is not inclined to believe in the possibility of change[9].

In a framework of social and territorial promotion, it is necessary to identify strategies that are first and foremost able to activate a series of social relationships, not necessarily characterized by solidarity in that, for example, through these relationships it must be possible to realize the full and effective recognition of the immigrants' rights. It is indispensable that they intervene in order to hold responsible political decision-makers as well as local communities and individuals (foreigners included). Therefore, regarding the recognition of immigrant rights, before ethnic and racial integration, they must work towards the generation of useful resources and activate processes of civil engagement: these are in fact absolutely indispensable for the building of public spaces of socialization.

Regarding multicultural social development in which sustainability and inclusion lead to activating social and economic resources, welfare must thus prevent and contain conflicts, but more than anything, it must do so by better regulating forms of coexistence, or rather caring for both the way of living and accessing the public space. In this perspective, greater commitment must consist of dealing with symbolic representation related to interethnic coexistence, or rather examining the logic that regulates the segregation system in immigrant housing in order to begin to change the way spaces of accommodation, inclusion, and coexistence are designed[10].

---

9   In Apulia, even the appointment of Prefect Iolanda Rolli as Special Commissioner for the government for the Manfredonia area (as well as for Castelvolturno in Campania and San Ferdinando in Calabria) does not seem to have produced any concrete results or social effect.

10   Fanizza F. (2015), *Lo smantellamento del gran ghetto di Rignano e la costruzione di un ecovillaggio per contrastare la riduzione in schiavitù dei braccianti immigrati della provincia di Foggia*, in Omizzolo M. e Sodano P. (a cura di), *Migranti e territori. Lavoro, diritti, accoglienza*, Ediesse, Roma. pp. 181 – 200.

By tightening the connection between solidarity and new citizen rights[11], this new welfare must keep in mind the need to fight illegal activities which the immigrants are often obligated to resort to for survival. As a result, welfare must carefully evaluate the abilities of the following parties:

• Territories, which must plan development;
• Immigrants, who must truly contribute to development;
• Locals, who must accept changes.

Rejecting the concept of the ethnicization of services, the constructing of formal and informal networks of locals, immigrants, public entities, non-profit organizations, and private companies must be a combination of evaluations of territorial vocations and the employment of individual abilities and skills. With the goal of improving everyone's living conditions, welfare must measure the range of its projects on the basis of the ability of social networks to elaborate and manage actions and paths within public spaces. Having surpassed territorial particularities, ethnic belonging, religious differences, cultural specificities, and individual political, social, and economic statuses, these new paths can promote services that serve individuals as well as affirm collective rights.

Assuming clear responsibility in managing differences and eliminating disparity, welfare must be characterized by the affirmation of principles that, unlike in the past, deal with matters linked to problems of social equality through the principle of equal opportunity both of individuals and territories. In order to improve social organization and offer adequate services to favour social integration, economic development, and cooperation in managing the *res publica*, the impact of recognizing diversities and valuing differences must produce results in community life, or in other words generate projects and approaches that consider the fragility of territories and the social vulnerability of the variables dependent on social factors and criticism, including illegality and criminal control of economic and productive activities/business. Only greater attention to the analyses of living and working contexts and environments will allow for the transformation of individual rights into the equivalent social rights.

The transition from "individual rights" to "social rights" is important not only because it is characterized by a change of perspective but also because this new paradigm foresees the encounter between different elements and subjects. More than mere and simple integration, welfare becomes a

---

11   Rodotà S. (2014), *Solidarietà. Un'utopia necessaria*, Laterza, Bari.

comparison, an understanding, and a reciprocal recognition that, inverting the logic characterized by "development without autonomy",[12] attempts to consider the recipients of social policies as artefacts of authentic lifestyle politics[13]. As they undermine aid-based and localistic mindsets, these lifestyle politics react to ways of understanding the State and the public sphere. An unaware-aware reaction that, in fact, can produce social innovation if it finds support in order to rebel and denounce the mafia mentality that pervades the economic, political, and social fabric of entire territories and populations.

12   Trigilia C. (1994), *Sviluppo senza autonomia. Effetti perversi delle politiche nel Mezzogiorno*, Il Mulino, Bologna.
13   Giddens, A., *Modernity and Self Identity: Self and Society in the Late Modern Age* (Stanford: Stanford University Press, 1991).

CONCLUSION
WELFARE AND COMBATTING THE AGROMAFIAS

FIAMMETTA FANIZZA, MARCO OMIZZOLO

I   In the complex framework of analysis herein contained derives the growing role of the mafias within the Italian agro-mobster system, considering this influence not only limited to the exclusive sphere of illicit brokering, of labor exploitation and, therefore, of agricultural production but also to that one of the large-scale distribution and logistics. This analysis confirms the penetration of the mafias also in the north of the country, in some cases facilitated by the structure of the two sectors analysed. In fact, they end up confirming their capacity for rooting in the traditional economic sectors and in all their evolutions. The actions of law enforcement and the judiciary have highlighted this process and the specific operating procedures that have been reconstructed. In particular, it results serious the persistence of clans belonging to various mafia clans in large fruit and vegetable markets and, in particular, those ones of the Municipalities of Fondi (Lt) and Milan. The interventions aimed at making the supply chain more transparent are, in this respect, fundamental, as well as a better governance of companies, holdings and districts confiscated by the state to the mafia organizations. However, it is essential to consider the capacity of penetration and also the conditioning of the social, administrative and political body of the country by the mafias, with proper tense relationship between their different sectors. The interventions produced, however, by the Financial Police in the course of 2017 in the Italian countryside, above all through the application of the law 199/2016, highlights first of all the operation of the same, the complex work of excellence of law enforcement, the systematic nature of the phenomenon and its link with the mafias, organized large-scale distribution and logistics. From this point of view, the recent declarations and political will of the current Italian government aimed at modifying this legislation and, apparently, to protect the production systems tout court, without some reflection and distinction on merit, end up underestimating the agro-mobster phenomenon, facilitating business and conditioning capacity.

II   The idea of using welfare in order to realize a social empowerment program represents an interesting source of ideas especially when illegality is the source of significant conditioning and the cause of serious problems. Since with immigration the problems are framed in settings dominated by violence and the violation of rights, the strategies of intervention must concentrate principally on the following:

- Identifying methods and ways for making political choices;
- Elaborating approaches that exclude an "emergency" mentality to manage problems of public order;
- Planning/Designing aid strategies concentrated on putting into practice the right of solidarity both of individuals and territories.

With the intention of ensuring better structural conditions to the human habitat, one possible way to combat the territories' criminal drift and the criminogenic drift of the conscience is a system of welfare that is able to oppose violence and the deprivation of rights imposed by criminality. Social empowerment programs must first and foremost combine active policies regarding employment with those regarding health insurance, education, and last but not least dignity and decorum in living spaces. On this point, combining dignified housing with processes to stimulate identification (or perhaps even a new identifying) of socio-cultural codes in both urban and rural living environments is a way to have welfare provide answers to a series of problems related to socio-territorial sustainability in various contexts: those so-called contexts "at risk of exclusion" and those densely populated; those characterized by elevated conflict and those interested in rapid processes of transformation.

Concerning immigration and the demand for integration/inclusion specifically, since the demographic movements and global socio-political upheavals represent a continuous challenge, the qualifying element of a welfare that grasps a multicultural perspective as necessary and inevitable resides primarily in a different cognitive framework of immigration. Compared to the classification of foreigners stigmatized on a basis of security policies (the immigrant as a "potentially devious subject") rather than an aid-based label (the immigrant as a "poor and needy subject") or a promotional character (the immigrant as a "subject to insert into the job market"), what is needed is a cognitive framework that allows public administrations as well as non-profit organizations and the various current and potential stakeholders, to participate in the creation of public policies or namely the planning of approaches and integrated services that aim at the confluence of responsibilities and skills among different or complimentary institutions. A different cognitive framework becomes crucial to favouring the involvement of all the stakeholders in the construction of different paths to inclusion: not only a basis of belonging (ethnic, religious, and cultural) but also in consideration of the specifics and characteristics of each nationality, biography, and context of arrival. In this perspective, welfare becomes an instrument for the following:

* Identifying new uses;
* Managing ethnic and cultural diversity on the part of public administrations;
* Coordinating the complex and transversal topic of immigration in local development policies.

Rather than sectorial and fragmentary actions, welfare should aim to introduce services to regenerate the abilities: of the immigrants, the unemployed, young people in search of their first job, students, institutions, territories, and all social participants involved and interested in various way in the designing of the future. Generally, only through a network of the different categories of stakeholders can the combination of the socio-territorial dimension and the various social participants produce innovative solutions.[14] For public administrations, these solutions lead to the launching of paths to growth and potentiality of economic resources as well as the recognizing and promoting of human and social capital.

With the goal of re-igniting community dynamics, the objective of welfare should tend towards a radical reconfiguration of public policies through an in-depth study of the abilities and skills present in a particular territorial, social, and politico-cultural environment. Thus welfare should stop handling social and aid-based topics and, above all regarding the topic of immigration, avoid proposing logics and territorialization/deterritorialization that risk, even if merely indirectly, feeding political marginalization.[15]

---

14 Rizza R., Bonvicini F. (a cura di) (2014), *Attori e territori del welfare. Innovazioni nel welfare aziendale e nelle politiche di contrasto all'impoverimento*, FrancoAngeli, Milano.

15 Regarding the scientific debate on "social innovation", see Klein J. L. and Harrison D. (2007). *L'innovation sociale. Émergence et effets sur la transformation des sociétés*. Québec: Presses de l'Université du Québec.
Moulaert F., MacCallum D., Mehmood A., Hamdouch A. (2013). *International Handbook of Social Innovation: Collective Action, Social Learning and*

In correlating the general renewal of the complex function of welfare with the idea of a reconfiguration of local policies, the perspective of welfare assumes a stylistic value, which finds in the words legality, rights, and equality the proper layout to promote economic development, social growth, social emancipation, and a free and pacific coexistence. The cornerstone for fighting widespread illegality and criminal power, the fundamental steps of legality, rights, and equality in a political administrative phase that calls attention on a European level first to matters linked to the relationships between the nation states, for reasons that depend on the ability of criminal organizations to expand, root themselves, and act in increasingly international orbits and with increasingly globalized practices. Precisely the decision to call *caporalato* an agromafia reveals the commitment of this essay to demonstrate how the reinforcement and international ramifications of *caporalato* concern the entire EU and EU agricultural policies, regulations, and the management of migratory fluxes. As a result, even the misappropriation of resources carried out by the *caporali* is a European problem just as it is a duty of Europe to continue to investigate and discover through which mechanisms the agromafias make profits and manage to condition all of our lives.

Transdisciplinary Research. Cheltenham UK: Edward Elgar; Leveque B., Fontan J.M., Klein J.L. (2014). *L'innovation sociale. Les marches d'une construction théorique et pratique*. Quebec: Presse de l'Université du Quebec.

BIBLIOGRAPHY

Agenzia di Stampa DIRE, "Sicurezza, fra paura e bisogno di immigrazione" (supplemento al numero 343 del 10 dicembre 2008, pag. 15).

Ambrosini, Maurizio, *Richiesti e respinti. L'immigrazione in Italia. Come e perché* (Milano: il Saggiatore, 2010).

Ambrosini, Maurizio, *Un'altra globalizzazione. La sfida delle migrazioni transnazionali* (Bologna: il Mulino, 2008).

Ambrosini, Maurizio, *Sociologia delle migrazioni* (Bologna: il Mulino, 2005).

Ambrosini, Maurizio, *Utili invasori* (Milano: FrancoAngeli, 1999).

Borghi V., Zamponi M. (2012), *Terra e lavoro nel capitalismo contemporaneo* (Milano: FrancoAngeli).

Colloca, Carlo, Corrado Alessandra, *The Global countryside:migrations in rural South of Italy* (Milano: FrancoAngeli, 2013).

Colombo, Asher, Sciortino Giuseppe, *Assimilati ed esclusi* (Bologna: il Mulino, 2002).

Cotesta, Vittorio, Cicchelli, Vincenzo and Nocenzi Mariella, *Global Society, cosmopolitan and human rights* (Soveria Mannelli: Rubbettino).

Denti D., Ferrari M. e Perocco F. (2005), *I sikh, storia e immigrazione* (Milano: FrancoAngeli).

Engels F. (2011), *La situazione della classe operaia in Inghilterra: in base a osservazioni dirette e fonti autentiche* (Milano: Edizioni Lotta Comunista, pp. 88-90).

Fanizza, Fiammetta, *Sistemi di welfare per nuovi stili di vita. Innovazione sociale, diritti e competenze* (Milano: FrancoAngeli, 2019).

Fanizza, Fiammetta, *Globalizzazione delle campagne e criminal hubs in Puglia. Le agromafie e le potenzialità della transformative education,* in De Salvo, Paola, Pochini Amerigo (a cura di), *La città in trasformazione. Flussi, ritmi urbani e politiche* (Roma: Aracne, 2018. pp. 67-78).

Gallino, Luciano, *Vite rinviate. Lo scandalo del lavoro precario* (Bari: Laterza, 2014).

Gallino, Luciano, *Globalizzazione e disuguaglianze* (Bari: Laterza, 2009).

Germani, Gino, *Sociologia della modernizzazione* (Bari: Laterza, 1971).

Giddens, Anthony, *Modernity and Self Identity: Self and Society in the Late Modern Age* (Stanford:Stanford University Press, 1991).

ILO, A global alliance against forced labour. Global report under the follow-up to the ILO Declaration on Fundamental principles and right work, Report of the Director general, International Labour Office, Ginevra, 2005.

I.L.O., C143 – Migrant Workers (Supplementary Provisions) Convention, 1975 (No. 143), *Adoption: Geneva, 60th ILC session (24 Jun 1975)*.

Kapezov, Yuri and Carbone Domenico (2018), *Che cos'è il welfare* (Roma: Carocci, 2018).

Klein, Juan – Luis and Harrison, Denis, *L'innovation sociale. Émergence et effets sur la transformation des sociétés* (Québec: Presses de l'Université du Québec, 2007).

Levesque, Benoit, Fontan, Jean-Marc and Klein, Jean-Luis, *L'innovation sociale. Les marches d'une construction théorique et pratique* (Quebec: Presse de l'Université du Quebec, 2014).

Leogrande, Alessandro, *Uomini e caporali. Viaggio tra i nuovi schiavi nelle campagne del Sud* (Milano: Mondadori, 2008).

Mancino, Michele, *I mali dell'emigrazione* (Casalvelino Scalo: Galzerano editore, 1988).

Mancino, Michele, *Lotte contadine in Basilicata. Le lotte bracciantili, il carcere fascista, Togliatti e la svolta politica in Basilicata nelle memorie di un protagonista* (Casalvelino Scalo: Galzarano Editore, 1983).

Masella, Luigi. (2013), *Braccianti nel Sud: una ricognizione storiografica*, in Mezzadra, Sandro e Ricciardi Maurizio, *No border. Movimenti indisciplinati* (Città di Castello: Ombre Corte, 2013).

Medici Senza Frontiere, (2008) *Una stagione all'inferno*, http://archivio. medicisenzafrontiere.it/allegati/pubblicazioni/rapporti/una_stagione_all_ inferno.pdf.

Moulaert, Frank, MacCallum, Diana, Mehmood, Abid and Hamdouch, Abdellillah, *International Handbook of Social Innovation: Collective Action, Social Learning and Transdisciplinary Research* (Cheltenham UK: Edward Elgar, 2013).

Nocifora, Enzo (a cura di), *Quasi schiavi* (Santarcangelo di Romagna: Maggioli Editore, 2014).

Omizzolo, Marco, *L'Asilo come diritto. Richiedenti, strutture e operatori. Ricerche e riflessioni* (Roma: Aracne, 2018).

Omizzolo, Marco, *Tratta internazionale nell'area del Mediterraneo e sfruttamento lavorativo: il caso della comunità indiana in provincia di Latina*, in Baldin, Serena and Zago, Moreno, *Eurospe of Migrations: Policies, Legal Issues and Experiences*" (Biblioteca della Società Aperta – Studi e Ricerche, Trieste: Eut edizioni – Edizioni Universitarie, 2017, pp. 307-328).

Omizzolo, Marco, *La lotta dei braccianti indiani in provincia di Latina contro lo sfruttamento lavorativo e il Gang-masters: lo sciopero del 18 aprile 2016*", in Galossi, Emanuele (a cura di), *Immigrazione e sindacato, VIII Rapporto*, (Fondazione Di Vittorio, Roma: Ediesse editore, 2017, pp. 269-282).

Omizzolo, Marco, "Migranti e diritti – tra mutamento sociale e buone pratiche", *Centro Studi Tempi Moderni* (Macerata: Simple ed., 2017).

Omizzolo, Marco and Sodano Pina, *Migranti e territori – Lavoro diritti accoglienza* (Roma: Ediesse editore, 2015)

Regione Puglia Deliberazione della Giunta Regionale N. 574 DEL 02-04-2014, Codice Cifra: PGI/DEL/2014/00006, Struttura Proponente: Servizio Politiche giovanili e cittadinanza sociale – Politiche per lo sviluppo economico, lavoro e..., Allegati: 574_2014_1.pdf (dim.: 210.66 kb – agg.: 07-04-2014), "Piano di azione sperimentale per un'accoglienza dignitosa e il lavoro regolare dei migranti in agricoltura. Documento d'indirizzo".

Rizza, Roberto and Bonvicini, Francesco (a cura di), *Attori e territori del welfare. Innovazioni nel welfare aziendale e nelle politiche di contrasto all'impoverimento* (Milano: FrancoAngeli, 2014).

Rodotà, Stefano, *Solidarietà. Un'utopia necessaria* (Bari: Laterza, 2014).

Sereni, Emilio, *Il capitalismo nelle campagne* (Torino: Einaudi, 1948).

Sodano, Pina, *Il Sahel tra crisi alimentari e flussi di popolazione*, in Maniscalco, Maria. Luisa, *Sahel in movimento. Nuove soggettività sociopolitiche tra globale e locale* (Torino: l'Harmattan, 2014).

Sonnino, Sidney, *Discorsi parlamentari* (Roma: Tipigrafia. della Camera dei Deputati, vol I, 1925).

Sonnino, Sidney and Franchetti, Leopoldo, *Condizioni politiche ed amministrative della Sicilia, 1876* (Roma: Donzelli, 2011).

Trigilia, Carlo, *Sviluppo senza autonomia. Effetti perversi delle politiche nel Mezzogiorno* (Bologna: il Mulino, 1994).

Van der Ploeg, Jan Douwe, *I nuovi contadini. Le campagne e le risposte alla globalizzazione* (Roma: Donzelli, 2009).

Zanfrini, Laura, *Sociologia delle migrazioni* (Bari: Laterza, 2007).

DOSSIER

Amnesty International, Volevamo braccia e sono arrivati uomini: sfruttamento lavorativo dei braccianti agricoli migranti in Italia, www.amnesty.it, 2012.

Amnesty International, Lavoro sfruttato due anni dopo, www.amnesty.it, 2014.

FLAI CGIL, Agromafie e caporalato, www.flai.it

In Migrazione, Punjab, www.inmigrazione.it, 2012.

In Migrazione, Doparsi per lavorare come schiavi, www.inmigrazione.it, 2014.

In Migrazione, Sfruttati a tempo indeterminato, www.inmigrazione.it, 2014.

Medici Senza Frontiere, I frutti dell'ipocrisia. Storie di chi l'agricoltura la fa. Di nascosto, 2005.

Medici Senza Frontiere, Una stagione all'inferno, 2008.

MIMESIS GROUP
www.mimesis-group.com

MIMESIS INTERNATIONAL
www.mimesisinternational.com
info@mimesisinternational.com

MIMESIS EDIZIONI
www.mimesisedizioni.it
mimesis@mimesisedizioni.it

ÉDITIONS MIMÉSIS
www.editionsmimesis.fr
info@editionsmimesis.fr

MIMESIS COMMUNICATION
www.mim-c.net

MIMESIS EU
www.mim-eu.com

Printed by Geca Industrie Grafiche, San Giuliano Milanese (MI)
in July 2019